ENTERING
LODGE GRASS

AN AMERICAN TIGER

Jake Jabs

An Autobiography

ACKNOWLEDGEMENTS

*I would like to thank my friend, John Bucci, a Marketing
Education teacher at Arvada High School, for his contributions
to the "Hiring Common Sense" chapter of this book.
I've spoken to John's marketing classes and DECA members
for 20 years, and we have often talked about writing a book on
free enterprise to be used to teach high school students.
It is from these experiences that the idea of writing a book
became a reality.*

*It seemed to be the right time to release this autobiography
during the Retailer of the Year 2000 Award at the
April High Point Furniture Market. I completed writing the
book March 18, and through the extraordinary efforts of my
team, it got to print on time.*

*I want to thank Andrew Zuppa, my Human Resources
Director, and Julie Naranja, my Public Relations Coordinator,
for their extra effort in producing this book.*

*I would also like to thank my wife, Ann,
for her patience and for allowing me the time to take care of
business and write at the same time.
Also, thanks to my General Manager, Mike Buscietta;
my Buyers and Management Team; my Buying Assistant,
Dessa Zamora; and all my 1,200 employees.
This remarkable group has made American Furniture
Warehouse the great company it is today.*

TABLE OF CONTENTS

From Small Montana Farm,
To Leading American Retailer

NHFA's
Retailer
of the
Year
2000

The prestigious Retailer of the Year Award is presented annually at the Spring International Home Furnishings Market in High Point, North Carolina. The recipient is selected for his/her outstanding contributions to the home furnishings industry, exemplary service to the community, and personal business achievements.

American
SUPERSTORE

FOREWARD

Jake Jabs' story isn't unique. It is, rather, quintessentially American. Immigrant parents who lacked formal education and never did learn to speak English without a heavy accent. A poor childhood, highlighted by extremely hard work and an extremely loving family. A rural background in a frontier backwater, followed by an eye-opening experience as a world traveler in the service of the country in the U.S. military. An ultimately successful business career borne out of naiveté, hardship, setbacks, fits, and starts.

Horatio Alger couldn't have written a more succinct tale.

What you read here isn't simply a rags-to-riches story, however. It's an educational tale of a man gaining wisdom throughout his life and sharing it with others. Jabs made all of the mistakes, but what comes across is not a just a story of someone who made good in spite of a world of obstacles; that would be obvious. No, what comes through here is an ongoing education and a willingness to help others succeed through hard work. He has learned great lessons the hard way and his strong beliefs are, well, believable—and honest—because he came by them the good old-fashioned way: he earned them.

Jake Jabs has become an icon in Denver through his folksy television commercials featuring all manner of exotic animals. Some people love him, others make fun in a condescending way, but they all know him to be just exactly what he is—a hard-working everyman who tells it like it is, and a man who delivers on his promises.

The Jabs here also shows through as a man who understands his good fortune and one who appreciates giving back to his community. His take on charitable giving, for example, comes straight from the heart and the head. It is better to give than receive, if for no other reason than the giver ends up reaping the benefits, in both spiritual and temporal ways. He says more than once here that he never got into the furniture business for the money; he did it for the adventure. The adventure continues, of course, and here in these pages it also inspires.

That Jake Jabs would come across the opportunity to buy out a failing operation called "American" and make it a resounding success seems more than appropriate. It must surely have been fated. His story—and the principles it founded—could easily give him the right to call his business "An American's Furniture Outlet."

The casual observer might think of Jabs as "that guy who wrestles tigers on TV." The tigers know better. He's one of them.

Jake at 10 years old.

PAPER TIGER

When I think about all that I have and all that I've been allowed—even encouraged—to accomplish in my life, I thank my lucky stars that I'm an American. It could have been so different and perhaps what could have been has made me so appreciative of this country and the Free Enterprise System.

My father was born and raised in Poland near the Russian border. His family immigrated to that part of Poland in the late 1700s—part of a settlement of Germans in Russia led by German-born "Catherine the Great" of Russia. The intent was for the Germans to teach the locals to farm. The same was also true of my mother's side of the family, who settled along the Volga River in Russia.

In 1916, the Russians invaded my father's family farm and drafted my father into the Russian army, along with a wagon and a team of horses. He was 18 years old. He never saw his parents or one of his sisters again. The Communists wrested control of Russia in the October Revolution of 1917. My father served in the Russian Army until 1921. The Russians refused to release him from duty because they desperately needed interpreters. He spoke German, Polish, and Russian.

My dad was an eyewitness to the Communist takeover of Russia. Nobody wanted to work. Instead, they intended to live off the government. Millions of people starved to death during this time. My dad would tell us horror stories about what the Russians did to each other. As a young man, he was a guard at a brewery for a time. The workers at the brewery had saved substantial quantities of seed grain. Fellow Russians attacked, slaughtering the workers in their attempt to wrest away the animals and seed grain. They killed fellow countrymen who espoused resentment of the Communists, especially educated people.

Lenin allotted everyone an acre of land in a move to stop the starvation. The United States Commission, headed up by the future President Herbert Hoover, sent food as relief, saving thousands of Russian lives, but, according to my dad, this also saved the Communist regime. My dad says that if Lenin had survived—he died at age 54—that communism would have been short-lived, as he no longer believed in its principles. When Lenin saw that Communism wasn't working, he introduced the New Economic Policy, a Socialist effort to entice small business to resume operations. Free trade was encouraged and foreign capitalists were invited to invest in Russia. Peasants were allowed to sell food to private customers.

Lenin appointed Joseph Stalin as General Secretary of the party. He began to doubt his choice and made overtures to remove Stalin from office, but died before he could accomplish his plan. History books report that Lenin died because he refused to take care of his health. He suffered a series of strokes and yet kept on working against his doctor's orders.

My dad remained convinced that Lenin died of frustration over the fact that Communism wasn't working as he'd imagined.

It would have been a different world altogether if Stalin had not gotten into power. History proved he was a ruthless killer, stealing the people's land, leaving millions to starve to death. Stalin ultimately returned the acre of land in another effort to halt the starvation, but he never reinstated the free enterprise system Lenin had adopted.

As far as I've been able to discover, most of my mother's side of the family starved to death under Stalin's regime. Most Germans fled Poland during and after World War I. The rest left as rumblings of World War II began. Those who had married into Polish families, of course, stayed behind in Poland. Luckily, my father's sister and her family escaped unharmed, fleeing the rumored Russian General reportedly bearing down on their community with plans to exterminate the Germans. They traveled by night eating grass roots to survive en route to East Germany.

The last my mother's parents ever heard from family members who had remained behind in Russia was a plea to not send further care packages. These consisted of clothes and canned foods. The Communists would descend on the family's acre farm and seize the packages and whatever else they could find, including seed for the next year's grain crop. The family was bloated and starving to death. This was pure genocide against the Germans living in Russia.

My father eventually immigrated to Brazil. Once there, he worked for two years to repay the fare for his boat crossing from Europe to South America. His aunt in Detroit, Michigan sponsored him to come to the United States. My mother's parents were acquainted with his aunt and the families corresponded, arranging a meeting between their "old maid" daughter (she was 20) and the newly immigrated nephew. My dad traveled from Detroit, where he worked as a carpenter, to Montana to meet my mother. They married in Detroit and moved to Montana to be near my mother's parents and start their own family. My father's formal education ended at the second grade level. He spoke broken English all of his life. My mother completed seventh grade. They always felt a little like visitors to foreign country. Both my parents—especially my dad—wanted us children to get an education, possibly because he didn't have one himself. All eight of us attended college; five graduated.

I traveled to Poland in 1988 seeking my roots. There, I rented a new car that drove like a used automobile. Manufactured by workers who had no incentive to perform, the car didn't either. The joke behind the Iron Curtain was "they pretend to pay us, and we pretend to work." Factory workers hide

Vodka bottles around the factory and drink while working. Imagine drunken workers trying to build a precision-tooled product. My father always predicted that Communism would fail. He called the system flawed. History proved him right.

It amazes me that Lenin's Tomb in Moscow is one of the biggest tourist attractions in the world. Thousands of people line up each day to view his embalmed body displayed in a glass-covered casket. Napoleon said no army could travel on an empty stomach. Russia couldn't even feed its own people, let alone a remote army stationed beyond its own boundaries. There was a time that Poland and parts of Russia were called the breadbasket of Europe. That was before Communists took over. In the end, the United States wasted so much money during the Cold War fighting a paper tiger.

Thank God our country is made up of at least a two party system of checks and balances. It prohibits anyone from becoming a dictator. That's what the Communist system really was. It's why I believe so strongly in the American system of free enterprise.

Entering
Lodge Grass, Montana.
Photo by Jake's friend,
Dick Ayers.

GROWING UP HARD

We were a family of nine kids (one older brother died at age 2, of diphtheria.) And we were poor, very poor. But we didn't know we were poor. We thought we were rich, in part because we were regarded as the best-dressed kids in school wearing the clothing our mother handmade for us.

Our home was a ranch outside Lodge Grass, Montana. Lodge Grass is a small town in the middle of the Crow Indian Reservation near the site of the Battle of Little Big Horn. As our family grew, dad moved a log cabin alongside our tiny frame house and cut a door to connect the two shelters. The five boys slept in the unheated log cabin. I remember awaking on cold Montana winter mornings and making a beeline for the main house. There, mother would have the cook stove fired up and we'd dress hovered around it. We had no indoor plumbing, electricity, or running water. The outhouse was equipped with a Sears' catalog; its slick pages served as toilet paper. We had two changes of clothes—one was in the wash while we wore the other. Our toys were bones from dead animals and our currency was pop-bottle caps. Once we attended the Big Horn County Fair, and bottle caps were strewn everywhere, completely destroying our familial monetary system.

The most important lessons my dad taught us were: Get an education (he always felt left out) and develop an art form or hobby (it would help in the tough times ahead.) Drugs and booze—other people's coping mechanisms—tear a person down; art and hobbies are uplifting, he always said.

My father was a violinist. It was a talent he claims helped him establish friendships in both South America and the United States even though he couldn't yet speak the language. Our family art was music. We formed a family band and played for country dances and special gatherings, me on the banjo, my brother on the guitar, my older sister on the piano, and my father on the violin. And we accompanied local school bands—I played in the Lodge Grass High School band when I was only in the second grade. Although we were poor, my father always managed to get us the instruments we needed to make our music.

The third lesson he shared with us was to not love money. This was born out of his experience growing up in Russia where he witnessed wealthy people killed for their money or stripped of it entirely. To this day, I maintain that one of the reasons I'm successful is that I'm not in this business for the money. Instead, I'm doing what I like to do. Money has never been important to me, something my wife reminds me of constantly.

When I enrolled in the first grade, my troubles began, in part because of my heritage. My father spoke broken English and people across the United States blamed our country's woes and our role in

*Jake in the
Montana State
College Band.
Freshman year, 1948*

WWII on Germany and Germans. I was expelled
several times for fighting, but it didn't stop me from
fistfights. That continued until I grew big enough to
whip most the boys who pestered me.

We sharecropped sugar beets. Producing a pros-
perous crop required that we thin the beets with a
short handled hoe, leaving a single beet about 8"
apart from the next. We streamlined the process by
hoeing the weeds at the same time. When we were
young, six or so, we'd see our mother hoeing the beets
in the fields. She raised eight kids, did all the cooking,
made our clothes, kept the house tidy, and still she
found time to work the beet fields. Even as youngsters,
we knew to offer our help. She allowed us that
opportunity, but cautioned us that we'd have to do
the work right and not give up after just a few hours.
It was slave labor, stooping or crawling on hand and
knee, backbreaking work.

We had our chores. One was tending to the
huge garden that mother planted religiously. Around
1937, a cricket epidemic hit. Hordes of crickets
would make their way through the valley, eating
everything in their path. The government assisted by
building six-inch-high tin fences to herd the crickets
into big oil barrels dug into the ground. The only
problem was that we were outnumbered—the oil
barrels couldn't contain so many crickets. As they
approached our farm, we'd wave blankets trying to

scare them off. Our blanket waving continued day and night. The garden was the only thing we saved that year.

We also helped with the haying. Horses would rebel when they knew they had a kid behind the reins and they would run away. We used horses for nearly everything in those days—plowing, harvesting, planting, and haying. Dad bought his first three-wheeled tractor in 1939; in our minds it was the greatest invention ever. With horses you had to get up at 5 a.m. to round them up (that always seemed to be my job) and harness them, feed them grain, and prepare to go to work in the fields. Horses added hours to the beginning and end of each day. Machinery eliminated that.

From the start, I was always bigger than my oldest brother. He suffered sleeping sickness as an infant, for which there was no cure. At one point, my parents left his bedside thinking he was dead. He was skinny, something I'd envy in later years. (He's now a State Senator in Montana.) Because I was the bigger child, it was my job, beginning at age 10, to stack the hay. We encountered plenty of snakes on the ranch, and every so often a rattlesnake could be found hanging from a load of hay. I'd wait until several heavy loads were dumped on top of the stack to ensure that the snake was finally buried before I'd go to work straightening it.

In 1940, we moved from the Little Horn Valley to the Big Horn Valley. As sharecroppers, Dad had accumulated enough cash to buy about 160 acres on the Big Horn and nearly 600 acres of dry land where we ran cattle and horses. World War II was underway and it was nearly impossible to hire hands to work the sugar beets, so we'd awake at 5 a.m., milk our several cows, gather eggs, slop the pigs, and whatever else needed doing. Than we'd work the sugar beets until about 10 a.m. When it finally warmed up, we'd thresh alfalfa. The alfalfa seed would bring 22 cents a pound, a lot of money in those days. We'd continue to work the sugar beets until after dark, finishing by 8 p.m. Looking back, I remember it as hard work. The boys would take turns deferring school until November, helping harvest the crops during those war years. Even colleges accommodated by letting students off class to help with the harvest.

The hardest work I ever did was to use dad's small threshing machine to capture our wheat, oats and barley. When we finished with our own ranch, we'd hire out to neighbors. Our pay for threshing grain for our neighbors was a load or two of grain, which we had to transport ourselves. The days started at 4 or 5 a.m. Afterwards, I'd grease the threshing machinery to have it ready at daylight. After chores and dinner, we'd unload the grain trucks with scoop shovels, laboring until we were dead tired. Then we'd cool down in the nearby irrigation ditch, washing the dust from our bodies. We'd finish sometimes as late at midnight and then start again the next day at 4 a.m.

They were hard times...happy times. And we grew up fast and responsible.

Jake and Rieny Jabs,
high school, 1947.

Three brothers
home on the farm in
Lodge Grass, Montana.
All three were officers.
Left to right:
Jake Jabs, Rieny Jabs,
and Ed Jabs, 1952.

OPERATION AIR FORCE

I graduated from Montana State College in Bozeman, in Vocational Agriculture in 1952. I'm supposed to be a vocational high school education teacher accredited for Future Farmers Of America (FFA). Probably the first inkling I had that there was something in the world besides agriculture was when I started teaching guitar in a music store in Bozeman. My brother and I worked our way through college doing odd jobs and playing music, and I started selling guitars. The war had ended and farmers had a lot of money. I was playing and teaching steel (Hawaiian) guitar in those days and a good steel guitar with amplifier could cost up to $1,000. They'd pay cash for this equipment and it was an easy sale for me.

The Korean Conflict was raging and my dad encouraged us to take R.O.T.C. He reasoned that when we graduated, we'd get a commission. I got mine in the Air Force, spending two years in active duty and six in the reserve. My three brothers and I served at the same time and each of us found that investing that little extra effort paid off handsomely. It was a whole lot better going into the service as a Second Lieutenant than as a private.

My first assignment following basic training at Hamilton Field was at a radar site, Point Arena, California. I'd head into San Francisco on weekends. Boy, was that a wild town for a farm kid from Montana. Filling time while I waited for my buddy to go into town with me one day, I filled out an application for top-secret clearance. (I already had secret clearance for the radar site, complete with a background investigation.) I was called to fill the need for top-secret clearance for the European Theatre of War, and away I went from New York to Hamburg, Germany on the George W. Gothels, used to transport military personnel.

We landed at Hamburg in the morning and had all day to spend shopping. I didn't realize that I could speak German until that day. As we walked around town pricing German cameras, motorcycles and clocks, I discovered that I could understand the shopkeepers. I could count readily in German. The time I spent in town with my grandmother in Hardin, Montana as a high school student paid off. She would talk to me by the hour in German because she could not speak English. My parents wouldn't speak German to us. When my oldest sister started school, the teachers discovered she didn't speak English, and they sent her home. After that, my folks did a complete turn-around, speaking only English with us. They may have over-reacted because it would have been helpful to be fluent in German, Russian, and Polish, with a little Portuguese thrown in. (My dad accomplished the Portuguese language while living in Brazil.) In a short time, I picked up more than a little German, and soon I had a bunch of fellow Air Force recruits following me around Hamburg using me as their interpreter. I was stationed in Germany for one month as I trained to be a security courier.

I was transferred to Nourasour Air Base at Casablanca, French Morocco in March 1953 where I handled all of the military top-secret mail sent to Africa. My orders allowed me to check out a boat, airplane, or armored vehicle to use to deliver top-secret communications, as I deemed necessary. My passport was stamped for access to any country except Soviet Russia and its allies.

I took a car along with me to Germany, something you could do as an officer. I had planned to motor through Italy, ferry my car to Tangiers, and complete the drive to Casablanca. I wanted to see Spain, and because Franco was still in power at the time, it intrigued me even more. I drew on all the advanced pay I had coming and drove down through Belgium, Holland, and France. I arrived at the Spanish border of Spain, but because Spain was a closed country, no American G.I. tourists were allowed. They argued that they wouldn't let me in, and as I prepared to leave, a man who'd been eavesdropping on our dispute offered to get me into Spain for $20. I was low on funds, but didn't have a lot of options. I couldn't travel the whole way to Italy because I was out of time and money, so I agreed. We drove into a canyon where he cut the border wire, and I entered Spain.

Spain was desperately poor. Crowds followed my new car through villages and towns, begging from me. I picked up a Danish merchant marine on his way to Gibraltar to meet a ship to Denmark. His boat had left him stranded and a Spanish girlfriend had stolen his wallet. He turned out to be a Godsend for me—he could speak Spanish fluently and could barter any price down. We ate like kings for six cents, drank wine for four, and stayed at hotels for 12 cents.

I had budgeted $6 to get my car across the Straights of Gibraltar. But when we arrived, the fare was $18, money I didn't have. This was before the advent of MasterCard, and I had to get my car onboard or risk being AWOL. I begged for money from passersby, and discovered the most lucrative place to beg was from passengers boarding the same boat. The Dane wanted a few T-shirts from me because he had no clothes. I collected enough cash at the last minute, swung my car into the hold, and it closed on my heels. I could hear my Danish friend's voice—it still haunts me today—hollering, "Don't forget the T-shirts." Too late, the T-shirts were in the trunk of the car in the hold of the boat.

When I disembarked at Gibraltar, the guards wanted a $4 dock charge to let my car off the boat. Now I was really in trouble. I was locked onboard with no way to get any money. In crossing, I had struck up a conversation with a schoolteacher and his wife en route to Casablanca and I had offered them a ride. They came looking for me and bailed me out. Besides no cash for the toll, my car was out of gas. The couple bought fuel for my car, and we set out for the three-hour drive to Casablanca.

When we reached the outskirts of Casablanca, a young Arab flagged us down and offered us directions into Casablanca, guidance we desperately needed. This was perhaps the worst place to drive I've ever been. I had to contend with confining European lanes filled with donkey carts, camels, and pedestrians transporting great loads on their heads. When the young man with directions departed, my passenger's purse was gone.

I had been on the base only a few days when a major approached me and said a bunch of the officers wanted to meet with me. I entered the meeting, held in a dark hut, filled with captains, majors, and colonels. Because I was the new security courier, they wanted me to fly to one of only two places in the world to exchange currency. They gave me $100,000 in cash and asked me to go to convert it to francs at a 30 percent increase. Because I didn't have to clear customs, I was the only person able to pull it off. Not knowing any better, I did what I was more or less ordered to do. They needed the better exchange rate to support their families.

I was assigned to the Post Office—there were five APOs (Post Offices) serving North Africa. A 1st lieutenant and I handled the five APOs plus a 24-hour mail regulatory center of 200 enlisted men. The Table of Organizations and Equipment (TO&E) called for six officers and 300 enlisted men, but because of the Korean Conflict, we were short-handed. The Air Force had built this huge air base equipped to handle the B-52 bombers that were kept in the air at all times loaded with atomic bombs ready to strike Russia quickly. I delivered the top-secret mail at that time and once mistakenly delivered an atomic bomb being transported from one base to another.

It came time to make out a new TO&E, so my CO asked me to make it out for 10 officers and 500 enlisted men. I argued that we didn't need that many people, but he said that that was the way they did it in the military. They always asked for more than they needed. The Korean Conflict had ended, so they sent the six officers and 300 enlisted men. It was a crazy time and I opted for an early out.

I've learned that a lot of government agencies operate this way: they inflate their budgets based on blowing this year's money or risk losing it from next year's budget. I've heard many similar stories and always believed that a good operation offers incentives or a bonus plan that under-spends the taxpayers' budget rather than wasting it.

Left to right:
1ˢᵗ Lieutenant
James M. Uptain, formerly
Jakes's ROTC instructor
in college, and Jake,
2ⁿᵈ Lieutenant, 1952.

Chuck Tombs and the Dixie Drifters.
This was the Air Force band.
They played at various functions
while they were stationed
in North Africa,
including parades and bull fights.
Jake is seated at right, 1953.

THE SECRET TO FREE ENTERPRISE

The secret to free enterprise is to find a need and fulfill that need. Then you're guaranteed success. Once I got out of the service, I played music for awhile in Nashville. I traveled with Marty Robbins and played lead guitar at one time. If I'd had the ability to sing like Marty Robbins, I'd still be playing music. The sideman's life wasn't for me, so I returned to Bozeman and visited every one of Bozeman's five music stores. None carried any good guitars, and the ones they had weren't in tune. In fact, none of the string instruments were in tune. It was in 1955 and Rock 'n Roll was busting loose. Folk music was huge. Glen Yarborough and the Kingston Trio were the rage. Everybody wanted to play the guitar. It was a natural for me to open a guitar studio, there was a need for someone who knew something about guitars. I was right. I was a hit selling televisions during the day and teaching guitar at night.

One of the partners in a store called Montana Music wanted to sell his half share. The recession was full bore and the store was struggling. I made a deal to buy his half interest and to buy out the other partner for $3,000 at year's end. We constructed a buy/sell agreement, and a year later I went to the bank to borrow the $3,000 to buy out my partner as agreed. The bank asked me for all kinds of financial information—statements, receivables, payables, and more. I had never taken any business classes and didn't have the information the banker wanted. My mind was racing. I had to have the $3,000 to pay off my partner, an older gentleman who hated rock and roll, country music and guitars. The animosity between us had grown increasingly sore and we were not getting along at all. The store had begun to boom, mostly because I was teaching and selling guitars, which were popular, plus I had introduced an accordion, piano, and organ teacher to the mix. We had a ready-made clientele with our students.

I was stocking the latest hit records and our 45 R.P.M. recorders and record players were moving quickly. Stocking the records meant we got the sales. The Gibson guitar salesman had stopped by and I ordered $5,000 in hot, new guitars. My partner had chewed me out questioning what I intended to do with $5,000 in guitars. "I'm going to sell them," I announced. They arrived and I sold them. It's called taking a risk.

It was clear the banker wasn't going to lend me the $3,000, so I told him I had 30 head of cattle and three horses back at the ranch. When each of us graduated from high school, dad made a gift of a heifer calf to us. That was eight years ago. The calves were certain to be more than enough security for the $3,000. Bankers in Montana understood ranching, but not small retail outlets. It's still difficult today to get bank loans for small business and that's a shame because small business is the lifeblood of Americans. Small business creates more jobs than any other venture. Most new investments and fresh ideas are generated by small businesses.

Based on the cattle as collateral, the banker lent me $3,000. When I presented my partner with the $3,000 check, he said he had changed his mind and didn't want to sell. He could see that business was beginning to prosper. His attorney had drawn up our agreement, so I went straight to that attorney to enforce our agreement. He mumbled something to me like "agreements are only as good as the people signing them," so I took matters into my own hands. The transaction was to close at year's-end and it was now 5 p.m. on New Year's Eve. I returned to the store and told the one employee she had to leave. I locked the door and invited my partner into the back room. I pointed my finger in his face and told him we had a deal and I wanted him to live up to it. He could see that I was serious, and he took the money and left.

I doubled my volume every year I had the store. I started to sell stereos and later TVs when they came into Bozeman in 1958. The first big volume I did was generated from a deal I struck with the cable TV company to purchase 100 cable installments at a reduced rate. I'd offer free cable installation with the purchase of a TV. It was a risk, but I was willing. I sold out the 100 installations in a couple of weeks.

The next really big volume I did was when Butte put a TV antenna on the divide between Bozeman and Butte. It was installed right before Christmas and people responded by buying electronics like crazy. My brother stopped by Billings to pick up a full truckload of TVs. As the only store in town that could promise delivery before Christmas, we sold 20 to 30 TVs a day.

My first exposure to furniture sales happened when I bought a carload of furniture out of Omaha. I planned to use furniture as door-busters; promoting sofas at $5 to the first person camped overnight at our door. People started showing up about 10 that night. I tied one man's hand to the door so there'd be no argument. His whole family joined him spending the night in front of the store. An Associated Press reporter was passing through Bozeman at 3 a.m. that morning looking for a motel room and noticed the gathering of people in front of the store. He backed up his car and asked what was going on. He was so enamored of the promotion concept that he put it on the AP wire transmitting it across country. Radio stations picked it up and talked endlessly about it.

I bought out and merged with several of my competitors until I was the only show in Bozeman. I did not purposely try to run any of them out of business. It just worked out that way. Some of the drug stores started discounting records and I was the only music store to compete with them. Soon they started hawking TVs, stereos, and other electronics I sold, so I determined to compete on these items also. I wasn't about to let them put me out of business. My business continued to grow until we became one of the largest music stores in the Northwest, doing over $350,000 annually, really big money at the time, especially in Montana.

I opened a store in Billings, Montana, a bigger market, and I suffered a rude awakening. To compete in the music business you need the good franchises like Gibson guitars and La Blanc clarinets. An industry acquaintance warned me that if I discounted guitars in Billings, he'd take away my franchise. He had been doing minimal business in Montana until I came along, and now he threatened to take my franchise from me. I couldn't believe what I was hearing.

I met my future wife in 1959. Ann was working for the bank and was sent to check on my floor plan. I had sold a TV that I hadn't got around to paying for yet. Because she was a good-looking 20-year-old, I took my time finding the TV. She returned to work a couple of hours later. Her banker boss said he understood. When I first met Ann, I was living in an old hotel directly across the street from my music store. It was a three-story walk-up without an elevator. My rent was only $25 a month. The rent included laundry service twice a week. Ann accompanied me to my room as I searched to find my cleanest dirty shirt.

I was scheduled to meet her parents in Ennis, Montana. Ann excused herself to go to the bathroom down the hall and the landlady accosted her. In that day, unescorted young women were suspect. And the landlady was every bit suspicious. When Ann returned, she said, "Boy, this place is a dump." I hadn't noticed. It was home to me. I was living below my means because that's something you must do when starting up a business.

I lost interest in the music business. I had planned to expand, but my hands were tied. Along the way, I went home to check on my 30 head of cattle and learned that when I'd left home at 16, the heifer calf had gone too. I had no cattle after all. I did pay off the bank, of course. I used to play music on weekends and ring the money up at the cash register. In the end, I sold my three stores in 1960 including Bozeman, Livingston (25 miles away), and the store I had opened in Billings. I retired for the first time in my life. I was 30 years old.

To this day, I'm opposed to franchises like Thomasville, Henredon, Lazyboy, and Bassett because of my experience in the music business. The furniture business is truly free enterprise. There are plenty of factories that will sell to you and you're not handcuffed, especially with the insurgence of imports.

Montana Music VW bus.
It was 1959.
This bus was used as a delivery vehicle.
Jake could fit as much as
three pianos and an organ in it.
Picture was taken outside of
the store front in
Bozeman, Montana.

HOW I LEARNED BUSINESS

I received a call from one of the owners of the Motorola distribution center in Billings. I was a Motorola dealer. He said, "Jake, you were always a good customer when you had your music store. I have a brother-in-law in Great Falls who is struggling with his appliance store. Would you run a sale for him?" My time was my own, so I said sure. It was a winner. One of the parties involved with the sale had a furniture store in Great Falls, and he brought in some furniture to supplement the sale. His interest was in running sales. He had the experience, so the two of us hooked up and started our sale business. When a sale was successful, the phone would ring with other offers to run even more sales for others. Most of these folks were struggling in business and wanted help.

My partnership with Bill only lasted for six months. We disagreed on several things from his banner that proclaimed "All sales final" to his policy of no refunds, no exchanges. I watched as he emptied out a store one night arguing with a customer over a $5 refund. When we split, I told him to take his sign along with him. At that point, I established the plug, "Don't argue with a customer even on a quitting business sale. Tell the customer you'll be happy to give them their money back." When we split up, my sales increased two to three times even though he was the pro and I was the amateur.

We had purchased a distributing company for appliances, TVs and records in Billings called Central Distributing Company. My partner had worked for Midland Distributing for years and enjoyed the business. I hated it because selling the appliances meant that we had to give the dealer 90 days of free floor space. We became the bill collector. I hated being the bill collector so much, that after 60 days, I bought him out, and liquidated the distributing company.

I ran the sales alone. Each time, I'd learn more about the business, meeting new people, and traveling to different parts of the country. Why did others need Jake Jabs to run a sale for them? There were plenty of reasons: owners who drank too much, some who were lazy, others with too many family obligations, gamblers on a losing streak. Most retailers just didn't have that burning drive to be Number One.

In order to be successful, you have to want to be the best in your market. Offer the best price, the best service, and stay open when your customers want to shop. If you do, a lot of good things will follow. You'll get better advertising rates, the pick of the best employees, superior locations, and most of all, customers start sending other customers to you. That's especially important today. You can't buy your way into business. Advertising costs too much. If someone sends you a customer, that person is partially pre-sold and it's a lot easier to close the deal.

The business grew. I had a crew of nearly 10 people working for me. I decided to make a deal with the store, buying the merchandise needed to hold the sale, plus manage the advertising. I did it by myself. To this day, I negotiate my media buys. You can negotiate a better deal than any ad agency when it's your own money!

EVERYBODY LOSES IN BANKRUPTCY

The moral of this story is nobody gets paid if a bankruptcy is forced. I drifted into furniture sales. I'm a believer if you need someone to run a sale for you or to tell you how to run your business or do your advertising, you should probably just get out of the business. So when I'm called to run a sale, I take a close look at the overall business assets vs. liabilities to recommend whether a retailer should go out of business. I've literally saved hundreds of stores from going bankrupt and was able to get them out of business with heads held high.

Joe had a store that once was successful, a nice big 40,000-square-foot store. He got into financial trouble. He owed $100,000 to creditors and had only $30,000 in assets, basically his inventory. He should have bowed out a few years sooner, but he didn't. He asked for my help, so I sent my best man Sherman to negotiate a $.30 on the dollar settlement with Joe's suppliers.

We had to get a sale going right away to produce the cash to pay the creditors. I was in the process of ordering two rail cars of furniture when I heard "bang, bang, bang" outside the showroom. The sheriff was boarding up the door and the windows because General Electric Credit Corporation (GECC) had reneged on its settlement of $.30 on the dollar. They had a judgment of $10,000 and the sheriff was exacting judgment. I went out to the showroom and asked the sheriff to show me his bond for the value of the inventory. The inventory totaled $30,000 requiring a $60,000 bond under the law. He could attach $10,000 worth of merchandise, but couldn't lock up the store, according to the statutes. He agreed with my argument and removed the bars from the doors.

GECC wanted its $10,000, and Joe and I agreed there wasn't enough inventory left to save the business. Bankruptcy was Joe's one alternative. Joe called one of the furniture suppliers he was trying to protect, asking him to send up a couple of big trailers. At 8 p.m. at night they started to empty the place of furniture. Meanwhile, the landlord was going crazy because he, too, had a $10,000 judgment. He kept circling the building trying to figure out a way to exercise his judgment. The sheriff hired a storage firm to haul out his $10,000 in merchandise. It turned out to be old inventory attached at retail price.

Because GECC tried to get their money ahead of the rest of the creditors, they forced poor old Joe into bankruptcy and nobody, including GECC, got paid. By the time GECC paid moving and storage costs, sheriff's process fees, and covered auction costs, they never got a dime out of it either.

MANUFACTURING HINDSIGHT

In 1968 in Bridger, Montana a factory called Lazy Bones was for sale. The factory manufactured mattresses, sofas, and bedroom sets. I had an employee, Ray Strickler, working my sales floor at Mediterranean Galleries who had previously managed Spring Aires plant in Denver for 17 years. The owners of Lazy Bones were having some financial and family problems. They wanted out of the business. Ray and I bought the factory, renamed it Yellowstone Manufacturing Company and decided to mass-produce that single sofa and love seat. I put up $40,000 in cash and he put up $10,000 to fund our newly formed corporation. We sold all the mattresses and equipment to get a large part of our interest back.

During that first year we just built one sofa and loveseat and wholesaled it at $145, netting $50,000. It proves that by tapping into economies of scale plus selling cheap, you can still make money. I bought out Ray in 1974. We renamed the factory "Loren Mitchell" in 1994. I don't recommend manufacturing for large retailers. It's too hands-on and consumes a lot of time. If I had to do it over again, I would never have bought the factory. I spent too many years nursing it along and too many hours calling on dealers and traveling all over the western United States selling Yellowstone to other retailers. I spent too much time away from my family. The reason I still operate

the factory boils down to the fact that there is something satisfying about taking constructing a nice sofa
out of raw materials. You create jobs. And the people
in Bridger, Montana really appreciate the factory.

The Mediterranean Look.

MEDITERRANEAN LIVING

It was 1968. I was running a "quitting business" sale for Howie Katchen's Mediterranean shops. He was going out of business because business was too good. Mediterranean furniture inherently had certain problems and Howie didn't want to deal with the customer service issues. During the sale, people went crazy for the Mediterranean pieces. I saw a demand. Remember, my motto is: Find a need and fulfill it and you'll be successful. So I reopened the store as Mediterranean Galleries. It was a high-end store featuring Thomasville, Stanley, Lane, and Bernhardt. I started importing out of Mexico. It was successful.

For my grand opening sale, I ran an ad for a Mediterranean sofa and loveseat at $199. I bought the goods from Sid Blitz, the owner of Sunline at the time, and I oversold 19 sets the first weekend. I immediately called Sid and said I need a truckload of this same sofa and loveseat bad. He stalled and balked at selling to me. So I took a snapshot of the set to five different Denver sofa factories and asked them to make me that set. I had been paying Sunline $144.95 for the two-piece set. The Denver manufacturers said it would cost $229. I said, "No." It sparked my curiosity. Why could Sunline make this set for $144.95 and the Denver factories ask $229? I traveled to Los Angeles and toured sofa factories including Sunline where I learned that if you build the same thing over and over again, you could figure out how to build it cheaper. The recipe was simple: Increase production, buy raw materials at a bulk discount, and put employees on piecework. Access economies of scale. Work on short margins. Sell in quantity to large accounts. You'll develop a successful manufacturing company.

Mediterranean lasted five years. I now operated four stores in Denver, Colorado Springs, Pueblo, and Billings. Nobody told me that Mediterranean would only last five years. I liked it, personally. But five years after its introduction, the style nose-dived, taking me with it. I pulled out all my best ads. They didn't work anymore. I had learned over my years of running sales for other people that many business-men went broke by holding onto a failing business too long. I didn't want to be one of them. I decided to get out of business before I went broke, liquidating my four stores in 1974, and I retired again.

The downside in any business is that it demands you reinvest continuously in that business. Buy more inventory, more trucks, more equipment, and new computers. You never have money to spend on your-self. I came out of the sale with some cash. It's the first time that I actually had any extra money. My wife was shopping several $100,000 CDs around.

We moved back to Montana and I ran the factory. We quickly revamped our Mediterranean stock to contemporary and traditional. Denver's historic boom and bust economy tanked from 1974 to 1975. Mangurian's was closing its stores across the country including its Denver location. The American Furniture Company was closing its eight Denver stores. As a farm kid from Montana, I saw opportunity. Historically, I've done well in recessions. It's when you can find deals on real estate and a lot of other things. So I decided to buy what was left of the old American Furniture Company. That meant taking over a 20-year lease on their building at $1 a square foot with no escalation clauses. They were looking for a successor to take over the lease. By taking over the lease, they agreed to sell all their equipment, trucks, warehouse racks, forklifts, adding machines, everything for $80,000 cash. I figure I made a million dollars the day I bought them out because the assets on their books totaled $1.5 million.

Over the years, I'd observed a few strong independent furniture stores like Nebraska Furniture Mart in Omaha, R.C. Willey in Salt Lake City, and American Home Furniture in Albuquerque. They survived recessions because they had deeper pockets, and thus could sell cheaper than the next guy. They come out of the recession with a lot of momentum while their competition would go out of business.

MAKING HISTORY

After buying the old American Furniture Company in 1975, I renamed it American Furniture Warehouse. I did this for several reasons: the warehouse concept was hot (Levitz was booming using this same concept), plus there was $50,000 in signage on the 180,000-square-foot building. I believed we could recapture some of the old American Furniture customers. Although I bought American Furniture Company in February of 1975, I decided to wait to open until after the April High Point Furniture Market. Clearly we needed to go to market to buy for this new store. Three of us went with the goal of buying a million dollars worth of furniture from factories that committed to shipping right away. The factories had plenty of stock on hand because of the recession. And because I had an excellent credit rating, C-1, these factories agreed to ship immediately. A good credit rating means that factories will give you first choice on special deals or closeouts because they know they are going to be paid.

We did $5 million in our first year and $8 million the second year. In 1980, we bought out our competitor, Vogue Furniture. I continued to buy out a few more stores and by 1984 we had nine locations. From 1984 to 1989, Colorado's economy spiraled out of control in the worst recession in the history of the state. Mainstay companies were shutting down by the day, moving their offices out of Denver. Our state led the nation in bankruptcy for five years. As a business, we were going down the tubes fast. When hard times hit, a quitting business sale by one store depresses the rest of the market even more. Stores continued to go out of business.

I lost money in 1984 and 1985, the only two years of losses in my business history. We were going broke along with everyone else. I ran my best ads and still nothing worked. I began to think that maybe it was time to change careers again. Should I go back to teaching guitar? That had always been a fun business. Could I open another music store? Teach vocational agriculture to high school students calling my college training into play? Or should I return to operating sales? I diagnosed my own ego trip. I had opened nine stores and that was something to be proud of, but I wondered, if I swallowed my ego, would that help save my business? It took me nearly six months to do this.

I went to TV to tell things like they were. "Things are tough in Denver right now," I said, "and when times get tough, the tough get going." I announced that I would close half of my stores, selling furniture at half price until my inventory dropped to its proper level. The sale was unbelievable. Clearly, people in Denver did not want to see us go out of business. They bought all we had to sell and then some. We cut the list price in half leaving us with a 15 percent profit. We actually made money because the sale was entirely cash and carry. Our advertising was word of mouth, and our other expenses were minimal. It worked so well that I decided to close five stores, keeping only those that were profitable.

I set my course at this time, resolving to keep selling furniture cheap. It's the course I've followed ever since. If you can do big volume, keep your advertising costs down and minimize your employee costs, run a lean, mean machine, you'll make money even with small margins. From that point on, our business grew dramatically. We are up 15 to 20 percent every year, passing up even the big guys—Levitz in 1990 and Weberg's in 1992.

Shortly after this, Weberg's struggled, selling to Rhodes Furniture of Atlanta in 1995. But Rhodes didn't do well in the Denver market. Their prices were too high. I had previously put together a deal with Rhodes to take them out of the Denver market. After Helig Meyers bought out Rhodes, the deal stalled. Rhodes continued to struggle, so we made a deal with Helig in 1998 to take Rhodes' eight stores and a large distribution center out.

We opened a few stores between 1989 and 1998, but just stores as the market dictated. Today we have nine stores. In 1987, I had the opportunity to buy a 104,000 square-foot building in Aurora, Colorado.

I stole it. Properties like this were things to dump during the recession. It would become our first super store. Our showrooms today are all 100,000 square feet. But as our business grew, we ran out of space in our 180,000 square-foot warehouse and showroom. It was 1992 and my lease was expiring. We sought a new location where we could build our dream facility, 470,000-plus square feet.

We rented a helicopter and flew over the city several times to select our present location at 84th and I-25 in Thornton, Colorado. That technique still works for us, and we normally do it once a year. I don't plan to open stores outside of Colorado. I believe you need to be the best operator in your market, offer the best selection, best prices, best employees, best delivery, best advertising, and best customer service. Do this, and you'll net lots of word-of-mouth advertising. That's what you need today to succeed. We will only expand as the market dictates.

We've now run out of room in our current 470,000-square-foot facility and are building a 635,000 sq. foot distribution/showroom. We made some mistakes in our earlier building. We didn't have ample delivery dock doors or customer pick up doors. Our new facility will have 68 dock doors and 20 customer pick up doors.

INCENTIVES WORK

I believe in the free enterprise system. I like to call it the incentive system. It's the only system that works. I've traveled to more than 50 countries and I've made a lifetime of studying different systems. I've determined that the Free Enterprise System is the only one that works, without incentives, no one will work, no matter if you're German, Russian, Polish, Black, White, Hispanic, or whatever. If you can pay people on an incentive program for what they do, your productivity more than doubles.

Immediately after opening American Furniture Warehouse in 1975, we struggled with our Receiving Department. Fifteen people worked in that department located at the other end of my 180,000 square foot building (4 1/2 acres). It seemed we had excess problems with this group–lots of turnover, fights, and drugs. I decided to institute an incentive system to stop those problems. I completed a six-month study of how many boxcars they could unload in a day, how many pieces could be moved by forklift, and how many deliveries could be stored in a day. I came up with a formula: pay a commission of 1 percent of wholesale, and that would total $5.50 per hour. That's what I was paying in 1975. I got all 15 together in my boardroom and presented my plan to them. I thought they would opt for the guaranteed hourly rate, but I was wrong. Two of them stopped by my office after the meeting and said, "Jake, we don't need

15 people in the department. We only need seven."
We transferred eight people to other departments
and seven people began to do the job. Now they do a
better job. They think and plan ahead. They earn
more when we operate more hand trucks and if we
install bigger platforms on the forklifts. They bring
us good ideas.

The biggest benefit now is that they are working
with the company instead of against it. It's in their
best interest to do well as a company. They prepare
for more trucks, and plan their vacations and days off
to accommodate deliveries. It's no longer a case of
company vs. employees, but rather, everyone on one
team working together to be successful.

If you pay directly for work completed, productivity more than doubles. I can open the door to the
factory and tell you if they are working on piecework
or salary. If workers produce more in less time their
standard of living improves on piecework. There's no
gossip about what someone did last Saturday night.
They are hustling because they are making good
money. At factories on salary you'll see groups gathered around the water cooler, and employees headed
to the lunchroom 10 minutes before break time.

To ensure that quality stays at its peak, you only
pay for top quality. Imperfect work requires that
employees stay after hours to repair it on their own
time. My chair-builders hate to stay after to work and

so it's a win-win situation. They do it right the first time. Employees take more pride in their work. Turnover is reduced dramatically. Our delivery drivers and helpers are on straight commission as are our deluxing people and salesmen. Whenever I'm able to, I offer an incentive or commission to employees.

I pay my delivery drivers straight commission of 1.5 percent and the helpers 1.35 percent. The best drivers make up to $70,000 per year. They have become very good at satisfying customers. We get lots of accolades from our customers about our good deliveries.

The end result is that they are more efficient and can build a product for less. That is the only way America can compete in the world market today. The American worker will work hard and can compete with anyone if given the proper incentives.

THE IMPORTANCE OF IMPORTING

I'm on a plane to Asia to attend the Singapore furniture show for one and one-half days. Then I'm off to Surabaya for two days where I'll look at furniture. I'll travel to Kuala Lumpur for a furniture show for another day and one-half and then to South China for three and one-half days. Finally, I'll head to Xiamen for a half day and to Beijing for three and one-half days. These faraway lands are where the values in furniture come from today. We do this every year in March.

Because of my parents' backgrounds I've always been a student of history and government. My interest in history and government increased when we started traveling to the Far East. I've imported goods since 1975.

Today we have to think of competition on a global basis. It seems everything is made somewhere else—clothes, TVs, VCRs, cars, computers, and toys. About 20 years ago, offshore manufacturers began to construct occasional tables. Now, the majority of occasional tables are made offshore. Soon, the industry began to manufacture items like jewelry armoires, hall trees, vanities, and brass fixtures. Next came dinettes and barstools, dining room furniture, and finally, bedroom suites.

One thing we need to do in this country is eliminate the 1930's Wage and Hour Act. At the time it was put into effect I'm sure it served a purpose. There were too many workers and not enough jobs, so the overtime calculation (time and one-half) discouraged employers from working employees more than 40 hours a week. Today our problem is the opposite. We've got too many jobs and not enough workers. We need reform.

I recognized early in my travels that someday the Asians would make everything. This, coupled with the large Asian population, guarantees it. They are entering their own Industrial Revolution, building everything for far less than we can in the United States.

For the past 20 years, we've bought our roll-top desks from Tech Lane in China, for example. The company added six million square feet of factory space within the past year, including construction time. It took us nine months to get a permit to add onto our parking lot in Thornton. We plan. They produce. The real beneficiary of our importing is the consumer. We sell a nice mahogany sleigh bed made in Indonesia for $799 while one of our competitors sells a similar version for $4,000. Once they learn to make any product in Asia, look out.

Asian countries can produce these items much cheaper than we can in this country because they have no welfare, they have no social security, no state comp, no unemployment insurance (we have both state and federal), no health insurance, no EEOC, and no OSHA. In an Asian country, you don't have to work through 17 layers of planning staff in order to get a permit to build a parking lot. Plus, most Asian workers take pride in their work, laboring up to 70 hours per week with no overtime.

China has 1.2 billion people, 70 percent of whom occupy rural China. Most Chinese peasants dream of the day they can leave the farm and move to the city. Besides China's 1.2 billion people, India has 900 million, Indonesia 220 million (the fourth most populated country in the world behind the United States), Japan has 125 million, Korea 60 million, Thailand 50 million, Malaysia 30 million, Taiwan 22 million, the Philippines has 50 million, Hong Kong has six million, Vietnam has 40 million, and Singapore has three million. We can bury our heads in the sand and act like they won't compete with us or we can come to terms with the fact that they can make fine quality furniture for less than half of that made in the United States.

China experimented with the Free Enterprise System shortly after Moe Toasung died in 1976 allowing farmers to free market their excess crops. China's food shortage under the Communist regime meant that they were paying hard cash for grain from the United States and Canada. They couldn't afford it. The Communists kept 50 percent of the crops, and the peasants could free market the rest. Production boomed. Soon, China didn't need to import grain. I witnessed rice piled up in the fields shortly after this new policy started. Deng Xiasping became Premier and traveled to Hong Kong and saw for himself this modern booming city. "Why can't we do this in China," he asked. So he opened up a free trade zone, just north of Hong Kong in Guangdong Provence.

It took off becoming a mini Hong Kong. Soon people were driving motorcycles and cars instead of riding bicycles. They built six-lane freeways instead of two-lane roads. In 1980, Deng announced four more free trade zones and they, too, boomed. Today the economy in China operates as a free market economy, by and large. The old Communist factories are closing as fast as they can because they lose money. When we visited Tianjin, we drove by miles of closed factories. We were told that they were former Communist-run factories. The Chinese government announced plans to close all of them. In these free trade zones, new factories, however, are flourishing.

Every year when we travel to China, we see remarkable change—new roads, new skyscrapers, new hotels, new parks, and new factories. The Taiwan Chinese, especially, are investing huge sums in China, as are other countries and companies. The Asian people love McDonald's and Kentucky Fried Chicken. There are 55 McDonald's in Singapore alone. In Hong Kong your can see five McDonald's from one street corner! Plus, these fast food chains continue to expand. I have to admit that McDonald's tastes pretty good after eating oriental food for a time.

I believe in free trade. We all benefit. The consumer gets better prices and can accumulate many more creature comforts with free trade.

Asian companies build cheaper because they have highly functional factories producing a single item or two year-round. They can focus on how to build whatever cheaper. U.S. factories are flexible, capable of making a variety of products, and often change the product being manufactured. Ongoing learning curves are inherent in a setting of constant change. As a result, quality varies greatly within the same factory and from one day to the next. Quality problems, wrong finishes, defects in assembly, etc., cannot be caught and corrected timely. Defective goods are shipped undetected. Retailers spend millions of dollars carrying extra inventory because we don't trust factory ship times. Factories should reduce the number of SKU's they manufacture, concentrate on the better selling products, and improve shipping.

Most Asian people work 70 hours a week. Factory workers in China earn $.95 to $1.30 per day. This sounds like slave labor to us, but to these people it's an opportunity. We witnessed people plowing with water buffalo and carrying water on their shoulders in buckets. There is a huge surplus in the labor force here, and with 70 percent of the Chinese people still working the farms and rice paddies, they long for 20th Century luxuries. Despite the low salaries, they save 30 percent of their earnings. Each year we observe huge improvements in highways, hotels, new factories, parks, and the way people dress. Six-lane highways now exist where two-lane streets once stood. Free enterprise works there.

China has no Social Security, no state worker's compensation, no unemployment insurance, no Medicaid, and no health insurance. Their cost of manufacturing is far less than ours. If we could get rid of just one of our own welfare programs, we would have so much money in our country's budget that we wouldn't know what to do with it. Medicaid has escalated into one of the biggest and most absurd welfare programs ever created in the United States. Asians don't need all these welfare programs because families take care of each other. No matter if you're unemployed, sick or old, the family takes care of you.

Jake checking out construction quality at an Asian chair factory.

THE AD MAN PRINCIPAL

There are plenty of ways to advertise your business. Small start-up businesses need to make sure they have new, good-looking signs. Amortize this expense over your term in business and it costs very little. The second cheapest way to promote your business is phone calls to your customers. Build a mailing list and mail to them regularly.

If it's a service, Business Yellow Pages are good. However, yellow pages aren't worth much in the retail business. Billboards work for motels, restaurants, gas stations, and services that people need while traveling, but they're too expensive for retail.

The big three I use are radio, TV, and newspaper. The choice depends on your budget and type of business. In the music business, I found radio to be effective. Furniture is a natural for TV, it shows product well, and allows you to promote sales event at the same time. Four-color print advertising has the same impact.

I believe business owners should do their own advertising. Outside agencies and promoters don't know your business like you do. They exaggerate and use adjectives that aren't accurate or truthful. They may raise money in the short term, but long term, you'll lose your customers.

The first TV commercial I made featured a three-piece living room group for $199. Everyone knows that for $199 you won't get a beautiful set. So from the onset, I determined I needed to do my own copy. Leave out the phony copy. Make it honest. Don't let the cameraman make the furniture look more expansive or impressive than it really is.

Also, I don't believe in "no-no-no" sales—no down payment, no payments for a specific period of time, and no interest. We make ads telling people interest isn't free and they believe us.

We spend half of our advertising budget on TV and half in print in one of Denver's two daily newspapers. We cut a super rate because of this competition. We opt out of radio altogether. We don't need to run circulars or mailings. We bought our own 1/2" beta camera several years ago, installed a complete advertising studio, and hired a full time video tech. We produce our own commercials in-house, as well as training tapes.

We started using animals when my wife and I bought our three daughters a puppy for Christmas in 1978. A puppy is the cutest and best pet of all, in my opinion. My daughter suggested I put the puppy in my TV commercials. We did and we started getting positive responses from people, along with their offers of using their pets in our ads. At this time, Glen Owen of Studio 40 produced our commercials along with other clients. He used some extra animals, including exotic animals, filming commercials for a

Lincoln-Mercury dealer. He brought one of the panthers to me urging me to use them in my commercials. I saw no connection between exotic animals and furniture and ran him off. Barbara Brown, my secretary at the time, wanted to pet a baby tiger and talked him into bringing a baby tiger to the store. When I came in to work the next morning, all the employees were gathered around the tiger. I was hopping mad because no one was working. But I saw the interest and excitement that the tiger generated. I started using them on my commercials and they've now become our trademark. People love them. We've accessed all kinds of animals from different sources around Colorado, but lately we get them from Fort Worth, Texas.

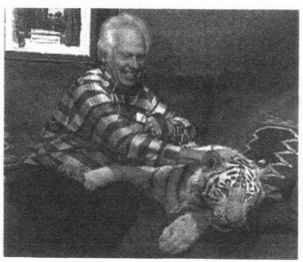

KNOW THY STRENGTHS

We asked our sales team to list strengths of our company. That list follows. I suggest all businesses do this. It helps to thoroughly understand your strengths, and you can detect your weaknesses and correct them.

Strengths of American Furniture Warehouse

1. LOWEST PRICES, BEST PRICE GUARANTEE

2. BEST SELECTION

3. BEST AND MOST ADVERTISING

4. GOOD IN-STOCK AVAILABILITY

5. BEST DELIVERY...ON TIME...
   7 DAYS A WEEK

6. CUSTOMER SERVICE...
   STAND BEHIND PRODUCT...
   HANDLE COMPLAINTS WELL

7. INFORMATIVE SALES STAFF

8. BUYING POWER

9. CUSTOMER SATISFACTION...
   GOOD REFUND POLICY

10. NO DICKER POLICY

11. BEST DISPLAYS...
    MODERN SHOWROOMS

12. GOOD EMPLOYEE BENEFITS

13. HONEST, UP-FRONT...
    INFORMATION TAGS

14. GOOD BUYERS

15. OWN FLEET OF TRUCKS

16. FAMILY OWNED...
    OWNER ACTIVE IN BUSINESS

17. GOOD MANAGEMENT...
    LONG TERM...
    NO MIDDLE MANAGEMENT

18. GOOD WORKING CONDITIONS

19. SPECIAL ORDERS ON TIME

20. BEST ACCESSORIES

21. WAREHOUSE PICK UP

22. GOOD MATTRESS PROGRAM...
    SIMMONS ONLY

23. GOOD COMPUTER SYSTEMS...FAST

24. FAIR TO EMPLOYEES

25. WILLING TO LISTEN TO CHANGE

26. GOOD REPUTATION AND TRUST

27. CONTAINER BUYING

28. LOREN MITCHELL...
    MADE IN MONTANA...
    OWN FACTORY

29. GOOD SERVICE SHOP...
    CONSTANTLY TRAINING...
    SERVICE TECH SCHOOL

30. GOOD, PROFESSIONAL
    TRUCK DRIVERS

31. GOOD TRAINING OF EMPLOYEES

BE THE BEST OPERATION

Colorado's economy has grown since 1990. We surpassed Levitz stores in sales in 1990. We passed Weberg's in 1992.

Rhodes bought Weberg's in 1995 and introduced lots of cherry, which doesn't sell in Colorado. Buck Thornton tried to turn Rhodes into a high-end store, but that didn't work either. Thornton didn't know this market. They put in the same line up as they had in Atlanta. If you're a big chain of stores, you still need to buy for the local market. Oak and pine sell here. Levitz went bankrupt. Fancy ads featuring an exclusive designer-leather product on the front page didn't work. It takes years and years to transform from a medium-priced store into a high-end store.

Customers need to know your position in the market place. The public is easily confused. They need to know where you stand. It's a natural tendency to bring in an outside expert as a consultant or to run your business, especially when times get tough or during a recession. I tried it a couple of times and it didn't work. They want to change your advertising. They want to change what you buy. They want to hire their people. It's not that simple. You can't wave a magic wand and turn your business around.

While I've done well buying out competitors, I did it mostly for location. Buying out stores to get rid of a competitor isn't a good idea. If you are the best operation in the marketplace—and that's the secret—the weaker stores will quit anyway. If you have the best operation in the market place, customers say good things about you and send you customers. Your advertising budget decreases and that goes to the bottom line. You can sell furniture for less. You sell more furniture and you make more money.

Also you get the pick of better employees. The salesmen around town want to work for you. This is true of everyone from the delivery drivers and warehouse people to salespeople. Good employees make a business successful.

I have had a lot of people attempt to buy me out and go public. There are very, very few successful public furniture companies. I can count them on one hand, and many of them go broke. Stockholders and Wall Street want good quarterly reports. They want earnings now, so they urge you to raise your prices.

The exception to this is Warren Buffet, CEO of Berkshire Hathaway that owns Salt Lake City-based R.C. Willey. Under his leadership, Berkshire Hathaway seems to be in it for the long haul.

EAGLES AND BOGIES

A musician friend of mine, Bo Cottrell, formed an entertainment company. One day as we lunched at my office he noticed a set of golf clubs. I had won them at a charity event. Although I had never played golf, he decided we needed to hold a celebrity golf tournament called the "Jake Jabs Celebrity Golf Classic." He pledged to do the work using my name.

I signed up for a couple of golf lessons. The day prior to the tournament, my secretary Barbara Brown called all the TV stations and clued them in on the tournament and the fact that I had never played golf. The suggestion took. The press showed up and ran news coverage of me missing putts and drives. We got great publicity out of it. We'd invited some big name celebrities—Leslie Nielson was one. The three-day tourney included a show Sunday night, golf Monday and Tuesday, and a Tuesday night auction. I acted as auctioneer, and we raised significant sums for various charities like Cerebral Palsy, Children's Hospital, and Make-A-Wish.

When the recession hit Colorado in the mid-1980s, I gave up the tournament. But it continued with other celebrities taking over—Gary Morris was one. Now it's called "The Bob Goen (from *Entertainment Tonight*) Celebrity Golf Classic."

INFORMATION PLEASE

Our motto is "Under Promise and Over Deliver." In 1975, black lacquer was popular. I used to go back to Return To Stock (RTS) and look at the merchandise coming off the delivery trucks. Among the returns was tons of black lacquer furniture. It seemed we were getting more back than we were delivering. We found that customer expectations were greater than we delivered. Our Budget Value tag was born. This told the customers that black

> **BUDGET VALUE INFORMATION**
>
> This merchandise comes with manufacturers' imperfections that are inherent in the mass production such as finish flaws etc.
>
> American Furniture Warehouse will give you its usual year warranty on the construction but cannot warranty the inherent imperfections.

lacquer has certain finish flaws. We trained our salesmen to point out the flaws at the time of the sale. This tag was stapled to the front of the sale tag so the customer had to see it, read it, and ask questions if they didn't understand it. Our problems with black lacquer went away.

We started tagging all items with finish problems. Brass was popular in 1980, but brass finishes were often pitted and not perfect. We found that by using the tag, customer expectations were reduced and we didn't get the product back. We were not returning flawed goods to factories as defective or giving them debit memos. In turn, they sold product to us cheaper than to others. We ended up owning the market. We continue to this day to tag items with cheap finishes. We rarely get returns.

Nostalgic oak was popular in the '80s, too. A five-store chain in Denver called Dreamworld sold solid oak. We sold cheaper veneers. A former Dreamworld manager came to work for us. I asked him how much solid oak they were getting back from customers. Because Colorado is dry climate, solid oak splits and cracks easily. His answer was about 35 percent, so I developed a Solid Wood tag. We began to sell solid oak furniture for 35 percent cheaper than Dreamworld. Shortly, they closed five of their stores.

Next came the Metal Bunk Bed tag. These beds are made mostly in Mexico, Indonesia, China, and Taiwan. Neither the Mexicans nor the Chinese ship in solid cartons, especially in those days. The heavy metal beds would be scratched en route. Again, this was a competitive product. Stores like Wal-Mart and Costco sold them. Because our tag advised buyers at the onset, we could sell them for less, get few if any back, and make a profit. Today we own that business with very little competition.

Our Distressed Furniture tag was made for the Broyhill Fontana Collection, the biggest selling furniture collection ever. When we took it on, the factory warned us that some people would want the dents and finish repaired. I said, "Not us," and developed this tag.

Next came the leather tag. As leather sales increased, I developed the Selling Leather tag. One large retailer wanted to send his delivery manager to me for training because he was refusing to deliver Viewpoint leather. He had heard we weren't having problems. I said the person who needs to visit is the storeowner and his sales manager. I knew the problem was with the sale not the delivery. I sent him all my tags, but they still don't use them. I've had dealers from all over the country visit us, and I usually give them tags. Few use them, but by and large they don't. They believe the tags are negative. But they're dead wrong. Customers don't consider

Rugged, Natural Beauty

it a negative. Customers are hungry for information about furniture and appreciate the fact that we are willing to give them this information before the purchase.

The Rusticos tag was made for the Rusticos furniture imported from Mexico. The hottest furniture selling right now is lifestyle light maple. The newest tag is Understanding Maple Furniture.

The more honest you can be with the customer, the more often they will return to buy from you

RUSTICOS FURNITURE

Rusticos means "Rustic". This furniture is made from native lumber in the country of origin. To give it the Old World look, it is hand made. It is purposely made to look rustic. In dry climates like Colorado and Montana, it needs to be oiled regularly. This furniture will often crack, doors warp and hinges squeak...adding to its appeal and value.

American Furniture Warehouse will give you its usual year warranty on the construction, but cannot warranty the cracking, warping and squeaky hinges.

UNDERSTANDING MAPLE FURNITURE

When purchasing maple furniture, it is important that you understand the nature and characteristics of this wood and the finishes applied to it.

Note the variations in the shading of the different pieces of wood and the different grain patterns. No two pieces of wood are the same.

Note the variations in the "birds eye" patterns. Each piece of wood will have a different "birds eye" pattern.

Because light finishes show the grains so much clearer, you have to like the variations before deciding to buy maple furniture.

again. Their expectations cannot be more than you deliver. Deliver more than they expect and you'll be a hero. They'll compliment you to their neighbors and relatives and send customers to shop at your store. Word-of-mouth advertising is a must to succeed, because the rest is too expensive.

52 INTELLIGENT REASONS TO SELL FOR LESS

The biggest problem in the furniture business today is returns of purchases from customers. A lot of retailers claim this is their biggest problem. In the past 10 years, we've had plenty of new folks who have moved to Colorado and shopped at our stores who want to know why our prices are so low. They tell me that where they're from—California, New York, Ohio—and they share with me the prices are much, much higher in these other places. They urge me to open a store in that market.

People generally want to know why our prices are so low. They want to make sure we're not selling seconds or clearance items. In light of this perception—a misconception, really—I developed 52 reasons we can sell for less. I make my salesmen memorize them so they can give the customer an intelligent answer when they're asked. They are, in order of importance:

1. We do not get merchandise back from customers. Our information tags and low prices reduce returns by 7 percent.

2. We direct import. We buy direct from overseas factories in full containers. Our buyers travel all over the world for the best buys! We buy for 30 to 60 percent less.

3. We do our own trucking. This saves freight costs and duplicate handling fees. We can consolidate shipments, saving 2 percent.

4. We sell in volume. We sell huge quantities, delivered and picked up from our warehouse, saving up to 20 percent.

5. We pay low rent. We own most of our buildings and negotiated great deals on them. We pay cash for land and buildings. No big mortgage payments, saving 2 percent.

6. We use better systems. Bar coding, radio frequency, and salespeople handling the data entry make us more efficient, saving 2 percent.

7. We use delivery agreements. Our customers sign the forms and accept responsibility for their delivery.

8. Our motto is "Under promise and over deliver." Customers are extremely happy when we do this. We don't get merchandise back!

9. We hire good employees. We have most employees on incentive plans because they do a better job of delivering, deluxing, pulling, and handling furniture on this plan. We also have a low turnover rate, saving 2 percent on training costs!

10. We pay our bills. Factories give us better buys because we always pay our bills. We often pay in advance to get the best buy and we don't rip-off factories with phony debit memos, saving up to 5 percent.

11. We are a privately held company. No stock holders demand high mark-ups and huge profits from us in order to get a big return on their investment. We are family owned and don't need big profits and lots of money. We can sell as cheaply as we want to!

12. We don't offer free financing. Interest is not free. We would have to raise our prices approximately 15 percent to give customers 12 months of free financing. Finance companies will only allow 90 days interest free.

13. We don't offer free delivery. Delivery isn't free. Insurance and trucks are not cheap today. Because we charge for delivery, approximately 40 percent of our customers pick up their own merchandise saving our customers money!

14. We buy newspaper and television ads cheaply. Our advertising runs less than 3 percent, 3 percent less than our competition.

15. We operate our own central warehouse distribution system. This saves the cost of duplicate handling and control systems.

16. We do not sell showroom samples. This saves on duplicate handling costs and damaged merchandise.

17. We do not negotiate on price. All of our customers get the lowest price possible.

18. We run lean and mean. We do not have any Vice Presidents, Senior Vice Presidents, or corporate officers with huge salaries!

19. Our owner is actively involved in every aspect of the business. There are no bureaucracies to slow down decision-making.

20. We build our own chairs. We can build them for half the cost of stores using outside sources for assembly. We save freight, repurchasing and reshipping costs.

21. We do not offer free professional decorating services. These services are built into the pricing.

22. We own one of our upholstery factories. This keeps other factories honest because we know the real costs involved in manufacturing!

23. We operate our own service technician-training program. Our training programs turn out master technicians capable of repairing and restoring warranty claims quickly, saving on even exchanges and large debit memos with factories.

24. We pay lower commissions to salespeople. We do such a huge volume that our salespeople actually make more than stores that pay double our commission, saving 2 percent.

25. We have our own sign shop. We keep the work in-house, saving 1 percent.

26. We have the best overall selection.
Our showrooms are expansive, allowing our buyers to provide customers with the best selection possible.

27. We have the best availability of merchandise. We drop factories that don't ship on time. This forces them to be honest if they want to deal with us.

28. We have our own advertising department. Our layout artists and video cameramen save us plenty.

29. Our buyers know what the local market wants and they buy it. We don't buy based on trends of East Coast customers.

30. Our stores always look fresh. Customers don't see the same old merchandise when they shop our stores because we change them often. If it doesn't sell, it's out of here!

31. We offer better customer service.
Our salespeople do not handle customer service issues. We have a full-time customer service staff trained to take care of customer problems!

32. We count on word-of-mouth advertising. Our satisfied customers do the advertising for us, saving us 3 percent.

33. We blanket ship when possible. We save up to 5 percent on carton costs when we pick up merchandise blanket-wrapped from the factory.

34. We perform our own truck maintenance. This saves on vehicle operation costs and there's no down time.

35. We do not pick up bedding. It costs $15 to dispose of a mattress at a refuse center. If we picked up bedding, we'd have to add that cost to the merchandise.

36. We do not offer layaway. It costs valuable warehouse space to store merchandise. Additionally, a high percentage of layaway customers ultimately cancel their orders.

37. Our stores are cleaner. Our salespeople play a big part in showroom upkeep. It's part of their job.

38. Our salespeople don't use high-pressure sales tactics. This creates a welcome, relaxed shopping environment for our customers.

39. We do not assemble Ready To Assemble (RTA) merchandise. Assembly adds to the cost of doing business because of the time required.

40. We will not store in-stock merchandise longer than seven days. Storing furniture costs us valuable warehouse space.

41. We recycle huge amounts of cardboard and paper. This improves profitability plus builds a strong community image.

42. We do not accept high cost credit cards. American Express charges too much to the retailer.

43. We self-insure our worker's compensation program. We can rehabilitate our own people without losing productivity and without employees experiencing a gap in pay.

44. We only pay on delivered merchandise. If we paid on business that's been written but not delivered, our salespeople wouldn't have any incentive to make the sale stick.

45. We have an in-house gym and personal trainer. We're committed to the long-term health of our employees.

46. We have an automated delivery call-in service. This saves on manpower required to contact every customer to confirm delivery.

47. We have our own TV production facility. We use our own cameras and in-house editing crew to save costs.

48. Our owner and his family are personalities on our TV commercials. We don't use highly paid actors.

49. We do not return merchandise to factories. Most factories will sell to us for 15 percent less than other retailers because we don't return merchandise or rip them off with debit memos.

50. Our buyers sniff out the smaller upstart factories offering the best value.

51. We buy accessories by the truckload from artisans in Mexico. The savings is up to 50 percent.

52. We train our delivery drivers. This save damaged merchandise and returns.

"From Small Beginning Farm To Leading American Retailer"

NHFA's
Retailer
of the Year
2000

WE DELIVER MORE THAN YOU THINK

I have always maintained there is no such thing as free delivery. People fail to consider delivery at the time they are buying furniture. They just assume it will show up automatically at their home. But there is so much care that has to take place between purchase and delivery that we developed a delivery agreement to help customers understand the process. We want our customers to be happy. And to achieve that it's essential they understand the extra mile we go in order to provide quality delivery. Here's what we tell them:

DELIVERY AGREEMENT

Please fill out this form to help us do it right the first time.

Date_____   Invoice #_____

TO RECEIVE YOUR 2 1/2 HOUR DELIVERY WINDOW SET BY OUR DELIVERY DEPARTMENT YOU MUST CALL 303-286-9331, OUTSIDE DENVER METRO AREA TOLL FREE 1-877-AFW-TRUCK (1-877-239-8782). AN EXACT DELIVERY TIME CAN BE ARRANGED FOR AN ADDITIONAL $30

		YES	NO
1.	Do you understand your 2 1/2 hour delivery window? (4 hour window for mountain deliveries)	☐	☐
2.	Did you know you will be charged for delivery if you are not home at the scheduled delivery time. You will be charged again for redelivery. If cancelling or rescheduling a delivery, you must do so 48 hours prior to delivery to avoid a $25 cancellation fee.	☐	☐
3.	Have you measured your home/doorways to fit new furniture.	☐	☐
4.	Do we have a map location and/or delivery instructions?	☐	☐
5.	Do we have correct address, apartment name and number on invoice?	☐	☐
6.	Do we have both your home and work numbers. Is there a cell phone or pager number we should have?	☐	☐
8.	Did you know we do not move your existing furniture without an additional charge? Please have your home ready to receive delivery.	☐	☐
9.	Any unusual things our delivery man should know? (3rd floor, narrow doors, sharp turns, security gates, elevators, new address, etc.)	☐	☐
10.	Did you know we do not move any electronics, TVs, computers, etc.?	☐	☐

You must have your receipt for refund or warranty
If you have any questions, please ask before signing.

Customer comments_____
_____
_____

I have read and understand these terms of the delivery agreement.

Customer signature_____

For delivery tips and mountain deliveries see reverse side

82

PARTS IS NOT JUST PARTS

Every furniture store professional I talk with claims that factories that don't ship parts are a major problem. Factories don't seem to understand the importance of shipping parts quickly. Shipping parts slowly can cost a dealer and the factory plenty in phone calls, faxes, e-mail, etc. The store can also lose sales and customers. The factory, in turn, can lose a dealer. Whatever happened to "just in time"? Colleges teach it. Customers expect it. Parts can be shipped the same day.

I toured Sauder's factory and overheard a retail customer call in for a part. The Sauder customer service rep had committed to memory all zip codes. When the customer called, she asked him what part he needed, said it would be shipped that day, and he'd receive it in three to five working days. The call lasted only one minute. She didn't ask questions—why he needed the part, had he lost it, how old was the merchandise, what had he paid for it—nothing. Therefore, she could take numerous phone calls per hour. I visited Sauder's Parts Department later that same day to see the part being shipped. If Sauder can do this on the thousands of items it sells, anybody can do it.

At my sofa factory in Montana, the "parts" we ship are mostly cushion covers, outside arms, and back pillows. Our policy requires one of the upholstery cutters to stay after work to ship the parts same-day.

We pay overtime. Our dealers are ecstatic. Factories like Sauder and Loren Mitchell already ship same-day parts. All factories should do this. It would save money, and make the furniture business more creditable to the retail customer.

Factories need to make shipping parts a priority. No delays. No putting the order in a file to be taken care of later. No questions asked. No checking whether the dealer lost the part. No checking if it's under warranty. No credit check. No factory reps going to the store to personally check on the request (that may take weeks or months.) There are no good questions, period. Just send the part. How much can a dresser knob, a glide, or even a nightstand top cost? Pennies. Yes, even the dresser top. Factories spend more time and money worrying if a parts order is legitimate than the part is worth. A dealer wouldn't order a part if he didn't need it. Plus, dealers lose parts. We order about 200 parts a day.

Indeed, paperwork cost more than the part in many cases. I recommend that the retailer fax the order to the manufacturer. The factory parts department then ships it the same day, taping the dealer's purchase order to the outside of the package. This way the dealer knows whom the part is for.

A piece of furniture lacking a part is in limbo. Either it is sitting in a dealer's inventory, not available for sale, or a customer is waiting for the part. Today's customer does not want to wait more than three days for a part. Sometimes a part that is worth pennies can cost the retailer thousands of dollars in problems and lost customers. Often the many phone calls back and forth, faxes, or customer exchanges can cost hundreds of dollars.

P.S. If parts are not shipped promptly, it is necessary to deduct the item from our inventory and debit the customer for the cost. We will give the item to charity.

FACTS ABOUT FACTORIES

Factories must learn to say "No." If a customer's expectations exceed what we deliver, we have a problem. If their expectations and what we deliver are the same, we're ok.

One reason that Sam's Club, Costco, and Wal-Mart are successful today is the customer enjoys immediate gratification. The customer buys it, loads it on a cart, and takes it home. Obviously, these stores can't stock everything. So if a shopper is seeking to furnish an entire home, it's off to a furniture store. The odds that a customer will buy from you go way up when their expectations are met. Factories can help in this by shipping Just In Time.

Factories should not book more then they can produce. Most customers will not accept a change in delivery date of their furniture. They feel deceived and want compensation for late deliveries. They are quick to call the Better Business Bureau and other consumer advocacy groups including media consumer advocates.

Factories need to understand that with today's electronic capabilities, the retail salesperson has access to shipping information. Stores like ours allow the salespeople to sell against incoming shipments. We cannot sell our samples off the floor because our business would drop 90 percent if customers can't see product. One of the main reasons we can offer such low markups is that selling warehouse inventory from floor samples increases our turns dramatically. And it only costs pennies to deliver furniture direct from the warehouse. Therefore, we frequently quote the customer a delivery date according to a purchase order. If that delivery date slips, we have a problem. Our customer has a problem. We have to call the customer and advise them that their merchandise won't deliver on time. This isn't acceptable to some customers.

I've quit buying from factories that are sales driven instead of production driven. All factories can produce merchandise. Because I've owned my upholstery factory for 32 years, I understand that it's hard to increase production. It takes more than a magic wand. To build a new facility, order equipment, and train additional employees takes time and money. I am still looking for the magician who is able to double or triple production!

Whenever my sales exceed my production at my own factory, I reduce my distribution rather than leave the factory holding the bag. Maybe another word for overselling is "greed!" It's time to just say "No!"

THE INTERNET MYTH

I can't conceive of anyone wanting to buy furniture over the Internet. Imagine delivering furniture to a customer sight unseen. Even using our information tags, our trained sales teams, our "Do It Right the First Time" form, our 110 delivery drivers, 60 service techs and 50-person deluxing staff, we still get back about 70 pieces of furniture a day, or about 3 percent.

Today's customer is fussy. Furniture must meet their high expectations, expectations that are increasing constantly. Consumer advocates–the Better Business Bureau and Consumer Protection Agency–customers will refuse furniture and demand full refunds in a heartbeat. Even **The Home Shopping Network** eliminated furniture from their offerings due to 50 percent returns.

Huge discounts of 30 to 60 percent are the norm on the Internet. But they're phony. A sofa or dinning room table that costs $400 wholesale can be marked up to $2,000. At 60 percent off, the customer still pays $800. We sell that sofa or dining table every day at $599.

The claim that furniture sold on the Internet costs less because it bypasses the brick-and-mortar retailers is also false. Someone has to stock and warehouse the product in order to ship quickly, which is what the Internet customer demands. Just ask *www.amazon.com*, which is now building huge warehouses.

No one can receive, handle and distribute furniture cheaper than we can. We have all the latest technology—radio frequency and bar coding. We have a huge warehouse. We have our own fleet of semis. We handled $255 million in furniture sales in 1999 and the figure keeps going up.

Major name brand furniture companies are refusing to have their furniture sold on the Internet for good reason. They understand that returns cost money and that delivering perfect furniture to the customer takes high-touch skills.

The furniture business looks easy to people who don't know anything about it. They believe they can offer savings to a customer. This may be true of certain factories and certain retailers. However, we at American Furniture Warehouse work on very close margins. We buy better than anybody, we handle furniture cheaper than anybody, and sell it cheaper than anybody, period.

Perhaps the greatest misnomer in the business is that the best furniture is made in North Carolina and that you can buy direct from North Carolina using an 800 number, or even the Internet. The best furniture and the best deals on furniture are not coming from North Carolina. They are, in fact, coming from places like China; Indonesia; Malaysia; the Philippines; Mexico; Phoenix, Arizona; Tupelo,

Mississippi; and California. For example, our Magic Wood Oak and Trendwood bunk beds come from Phoenix, from factories that are low-cost producers. Arizona regularly produces products for less. And because we buy heavily and don't return merchandise, they sell to us for less.

The best home office is now made in California or Mexico. The best wrought iron is made in Indonesia and Mexico. The best-valued living room furniture is made in Mississippi and Tennessee. The best bedroom and dining room furniture is made in Asia. Almost all occasional tables are made in the Far East. We consume 60 percent of the local Simmons Factory production.

The idea that the Internet can reach out and buy in bulk, and therefore pass the savings on to the customer, might work well with some commodities, but the furniture business already does that right in your own back yard. You get the savings right here, you get the knowledge right here and, we back it up right here.

DOING LUNCH

I hold a five-hour lunch with every new employee. I do it in groups of five or more individuals at least twice a month. That's so employees get orientated before they have been employed too long. The purpose of these meetings is to tell our story. We let our employees in on our way of doing business so that we are all headed down the same road.

I start by distributing our personnel policies. I stress that our main desire is to be the best operation in the marketplace. Their role in this is very important because they are the ones who deal with the customers.

I then go over our sexual harassment policy. I talk about gossip and rumor, and that these two elements tear a company down. False accusations can injure a person for life. I advise them that if there's a harassment problem, they are to send it to us in upper management. We will send in a SWAT team to take care of it. We have zero-tolerance when it comes to sexual harassment.

Next I address drugs. I don't waiver on this. I am adamantly opposed to drugs. I watched it destroy people's lives when I was playing music. To ensure that we remain drug free, we drug test every one as a pre-employment requirement. Then we randomly test all employees. Fifty-eight percent of the people in this country in jails are in because of a drug-related charge. We just traveled to Singapore and Malaysia where we saw signs warning "Death to Drug Traffickers." They have no drug problems. You can walk the streets at 2 a.m. and feel perfectly safe. Most countries don't tolerate drugs. Asian and Muslim countries especially– which comprise a huge part of the world's population– don't tolerate drugs. We'd be better off in this country if we didn't tolerate drugs either. We'll try and do our part at this company. We are determined to be a drug-free company.

Then I review worker's compensation. We self-insure our worker's comp package, a move that gives us an incentive to have a safe work place. We have a safety committee to investigate all accidents. We put the $500,000 a year we save back into the business to have the safest working conditions possible. Everyone loses with a workplace accident, so we do everything we can, every day, to ensure that it doesn't happen here.

I go over promotions and transfers. I believe in promoting from within. All managers at American Furniture Warehouse started in positions similar to those new employees attending my luncheon. I don't believe in bringing in experts to screw up our business.

I review our evaluation and promotion policy. I stress that managers have to earn the right to fire someone. People here cannot be fired indiscriminately. We have a review system and employees need to receive one or more warnings in writing before they can be fired.

I emphasize that new employees will always get a fair hearing at American Furniture Warehouse because co-workers don't become CEOs, Human Resource Directors, or Managers unless they are fair. I review the salesmen job description. Our mission is to exceed customers' expectations. If customers expect more than we deliver, it costs us a lot of money plus it disappoints the customer. Our motto is "Under promise and over deliver." We're honest. We tolerate no high-pressure selling. We give customers their money back. Every employee—new or otherwise—can offer a refund to a customer.

The job description for salesperson at American Furniture Warehouse is 16 pages long. We address every conceivable problem that might arise as we sell and deliver furniture. Salespeople are assigned certain areas of the store to keep clean. Today you must have clean stores. We spend a lot of time on our information tags so that everyone, including delivery drivers, office personnel, customer service, and salespeople understand our information tags.

We train our salespeople to respond with a big loud "no" to customers who ask for a discount, free delivery, or other special favors. Salespeople are not to ask their managers for anything. NO. We sell at only one price. No negotiation. This helps us run our stores using significantly fewer managers. It keeps us lean and mean.

We review our delivery system so that they can explain it to our customers. We train to measure large pieces because they can cause big problems when being delivered if not measured properly.

Finally, I address our grievance policy. I ask the new employees why it is that we have such a policy, and they usually come back with comments like "stops lawsuits," "fairness to employees," "protects the job". While those things are all true, a good grievance policy keeps the unions out. We're an anti-union company. That's because we had a union from 1975 until 1978. When I started American Furniture Warehouse in 1975, I had hired some of the former American employees. This was a mistake because the old American had four unions. Unions often prey on start-up companies. We didn't have good benefits, 401(k) retirement plans, eyeglasses insurance, etc. because I had put every penny I had into getting the company going. The employees held a union election and I lost, something I should have taken more seriously than I did. While negotiating the contract, union reps said that if I would agree to two things—debiting the employee union dues from their paychecks and running a closed shop—I could write the contact myself and basically set salaries. I decided at that time that the union really didn't care about the employees. During the three years we had the union, union stewards never entered our stores—in other words, they did nothing for the employees. Union demands for a closed shop meant that all employees had to join the union. This put us at a disadvantage. Our competition wasn't union. We were the only union furniture store in Colorado and those younger employees who didn't want to join the union walked because they didn't like the union seniority system.

I appreciate a level playing field, something that's absent in a union atmosphere. And it's harder to get rid of a union, too. It takes three-quarters of the employees to go to the National Labor Relations Board (NRLB) to petition for a new election; it takes only 51 percent to have the first election. It's difficult to get three-quarters of your employees to go down to the NRLB. When the union anticipated they would lose the election, they pulled a wild cat strike. They hired professional picketers, toting signs emblazoned with "American cheats its employees" at both of our entrances. These picketers stopped all customers, giving them a handbill with the same criticisms. Only one of my employees joined the picket line for a half day. The remainder of the time, union-hired picketers walked the line. Unions try to bully you into signing a union contract. If customers won't break through the picket line, you are a dead duck, especially in towns like Butte, Montana and Detroit, Michigan, both heavily unionized towns.

Fortunately Denver is not a union town, and our customers shopped with us despite the pickets. We won the battle. The union picketed for about two weeks and finally gave up. We held an election that I won. I've had a total of four elections in all. Our grievance policy helped win the union elections. It's important for an employer to meet with employees in separate meetings. It gives the employer opportunity to listen. The union's big lie is that it claims to listen to employees and to give them what they want.

In the end, the five-hour power luncheon with new employees is often exhausting, but it illustrates that we mean business. New employees exit the meeting with an improved understanding of our business, the effort we've put into mastering it, and the time we're willing to invest in each of them individually so that they might prosper at American. They appreciate it.

HIRING COMMON SENSE

Something I've learned over the years that never ceases to amaze me are the unnecessary problems employees create for themselves and their employers by not exercising simple common sense on the job. Young and old, experienced and inexperienced, many employees develop problems that stem from poor judgment, usually caused by a lack of common sense on the job, a lack of training before and during the early stages of employment, and a lack of understanding of what it takes to keep the customer happy. Think about it. An awful lot of employee problems are the direct result of lack of common sense; not lack of skill and ability. A few situations that common sense and/or a lack of it could help or hurt a business include:

TELEPHONE USE—Use proper telephone manners. Too often employees feel that since a customer cannot see them over the phone, it's acceptable to lower the level of customer service. Not true. Don't leave a customer on hold too long. Avoid making and receiving unnecessary personal calls while on the job.

OPENING AND CLOSING—Arrive early and plan on staying a few minutes later than scheduled. Confirm that housekeeping chores are done before customers arrive and at the end of the business day.

ARRIVE ON TIME—Show up late; get fired! Tardiness may result in a loss of promotion, loss of a raise, loss

97

of trust on your part, possible loss of business, and a loss of the job.

BE COURTEOUS-That includes anyone who enters the store-customers, fellow employees, management, and manufacturer's reps.

FRIENDS—I don't mind employee's friends in the store if they are there as legitimate customers. But friends who stop by to distract my employees are not good for business. Customers get upset when employees aren't waiting on them. And fellow employees resent it too.

INITIATIVE—Show it. Ask questions, but not unnecessary ones. This is one way to show potential.

BREAKS—Keep them on track. Common sense would tell an employee that he/she doesn't have time to leave the store to run errands within the allotted lunchtime.

Over the years I have seen my share of employees who don't place much importance on fulfilling their responsibilities when they are scheduled to work. Of course, these employees usually don't last long, but it is best if these types of problems don't occur in the first place. Employee absenteeism and tardiness can adversely impact a business. Training can address this before it becomes a problem. Convey to employees that they need a valid reason to miss work. A minor headache shouldn't keep them home. Relations between management and employees and even co-workers become strained because of excessive absences and tardiness.

Being dishonest about being sick results in disciplinary action or termination.

If an employee is ill, the more notice we have that he/she won't be coming in, the better. Excessive absence and tardiness causes resentment, lack of cooperation, and lack of trust. Others may have to do twice the work to make up for the absent employee. Excellent attendance and punctuality build a good work record.

I pay my employees a fair and competitive wage. In fact, the pay scale in my stores is consistently higher than those of my competitors. In return, I expect a fair day's work by my employees. A lot of things work against business—competition, employee theft, bad checks, and non-collectable credit debt, just to name a few. These are obvious concerns to all businesspeople. But many business owners and managers aren't aware of a culprit that is robbing them blind—"Time Theft." It's the intentional waste and misuse of time on the job. When time is wasted, production is affected. Time theft happens constantly in business. There is no way I could ever eliminate it in my stores.

But with proper training, I try to keep it to a minimum. Communicate to your people what you expect of them during their early stages of employment. Time stealers include arriving to work late and leaving early. Ten full-time employees who arrive to work late five minutes a day, five days a week, will waste 250 minutes a week, 1,000 minutes a month, and 12,000 minutes a year. That's 200 hours. Add to that the time stolen when employees sneaking out a little early and you compound the problem. Also habitually long lunch and dinner breaks add up. The 30-minute lunch break that turns into the 45-minute lunch break costs businesses money. Finally, excessive socializing with fellow employees is costly.

THE MAKING OF A SALESPERSON

t American Furniture Warehouse we're thorough. Perhaps that's nowhere more evident than in our job description for our sales team. These are the people who interact with our customers. They drive our business and our reputation. Our job description for this key position is 16 pages long, reprinted here:

SALES CONSULTANT JOB DESCRIPTION AND STORE POLICY MANUAL

American Furniture Warehouse is a consumer-oriented business. It is of primary importance that its employees realize their roles in the area of public relations. This is important to the satisfaction of the consumer, your fellow employees, and to management. Our main desire is to be the best operation in the marketplace.

Your evaluation as an employee does not end with the customer or your job duties. It also includes your ability to work well with your associates and with the management of the organization. Your overall attitude as a positive morale boosting individual and your desire to improve yourself are of equal importance. We are a people-oriented business. There is a need for you to always remember your role in this regard.

The customer should have a clear understanding at the point of sale about the merchandise purchased, delivery procedures, dock pick-up procedures, what is involved in special orders, if they are purchasing a floor sample, if they are buying budget value, etc. The customer must know at the point of sale about budget value furniture, Ready To Assemble furniture and that they will be charged a re-delivery charge if they are not home for scheduled delivery, etc. It is your responsibility to discuss these points with the customer. You must check inventory and know the status of what you are selling the customer. You may not have fully earned your commission if policies outlined in this manual are not followed.

RESPONSIBILITIES OF A SALES CONSULTANT

1. No profanity! No alcohol! No drugs! while on the premises or prior to your shift.

2. All sales consultants are required to meet a $40,000 monthly quota. Not meeting the quota in a 90-day continuous period will result in personnel action including suspension or termination of employment.

3. Sales consultants are to have a copy of the "Sales Consultant Job Description and Store Policy Manual" readily available at all times.

4. Sales consultants must have a pen, tape measure, calculator, nametag, and Duro-frame catalog with them at all times.

5. All sales consultants must report 30 minutes prior to their shift for a brief sales meeting and to clean their assigned areas. Attendance at all scheduled sales and product meetings is mandatory. The Saturday sales meeting begins promptly at 9:00 a.m. every Saturday.

6. Tardiness and absenteeism will not be tolerated except in the case of proven illness, injury or accident. Pre-approval of tardiness is solely the discretion of the Sales Manager or Store Manager. We expect sales consultants to be at work on time and to arrange their time and affairs accordingly. If you are going to be late, call your supervisor. A doctor's excuse is required for missing extremely busy days such as Saturdays, Sundays or holidays.

7. Lunch hours are a maximum of one hour. Consultants are required to punch in and out on the time clock for meal breaks, even if you remain on property.

8. No personal phone calls from the showroom phones, incoming or outgoing, except in an emergency.

9. All sales consultants are required to work on holidays.
   Martin Luther King's Birthday, Presidents Day, Memorial Day, Independence Day, Labor Day,

Columbus Day, Veterans Day, Day After
Thanksgiving, Day After Christmas, and New
Year's Day.

10. Do not ask to be released early from your shift.
All customers are important and need to be
waited on promptly. You are not to leave before
your scheduled shift is over.

11. All sales consultants are required to aid in the
tagging of merchandise when price changes
occur. Tagging will be done before or after store
hours to maximize your sales opportunities. All
sales consultants must report to work one our
prior to their shift on retagging days. See your
manager for those days.

12. Customers like shopping in a clean well displayed
store. Our showrooms are very large and it is
impossible for our display and cleaning personnel
to keep them looking nice. All cleaning assignments
are subject to change at the manager's discretion.

• Keep vacuumed, dusted, cleaned and displayed
properly (e.g. straighten pillows, etc.) on a
daily basis.

• Check all tags--information tags and price tags.
It is the responsibility of the sales person to
replace all missing tags in their assigned area.
Report mistakenly tagged merchandise immediately

to the Sales Manager, Store Manager or
Staging Manager.

• Notify the Sales Manager, Buyer or Merchandise
Manager in writing of any defective or damaged
merchandise so it can be repaired, or put it in the
floor repair book. Discovering defective
merchandise during your sales presentation
discredits your sales efforts.

• Keep yourself informed of any changes of
merchandise both going out and coming in on
display in your area of responsibility. Inform
other consultants of these changes.

• Check all out of stock tags and sold tags located
in your area.

13. Sales consultants are required to spend time
answering all incoming phone calls promptly and
courteously. If a customer's questions cannot be
answered immediately, get their name and phone
number and call them back as soon as possible.

14. When paging "available sales," state the floor
area that is being questioned (Simmons, dinettes,
etc.). These pages need to be answered as soon as
possible by any sales consultant on the show floor.

15. In order to fully earn your commission you are
required to send out a minimum of seven thank
you cards a day. American Furniture Warehouse
supplies these cards and postage.

16. Invoice errors will be the responsibility of the sales consultants writing and keying the invoice and shall be treated as such. You may not have fully earned your commission if invoice errors are made. Continuous errors could result in suspension or termination.

17. Main store sales consultants are not to sell merchandise from satellite store floors or satellite store warehouses. Satellite store sales consultants are also not allowed to sell from other satellite store floors or satellite store warehouses. Sales consultants are not permitted to call other stores searching for merchandise or give the customer stock quantities at other satellite store locations.

18. Sales consultants can better themselves by shopping other companies, comparing prices, displays, etc. They can then speak with confidence about our lower pricing. Shopping reports need to be filled out and returned to your Store Manager so this information can be shared with others. Sales consultants are required to produce shopping reports monthly.

19. Watch for customers switching tags. Make sure the item you are selling is what is printed on the price tag. Make sure all tags are attached to the merchandise. If you're not sure or a tag is missing, look at the price tags on other matching pieces,

get the vendor name, and always check the SKU book. All accessories have model numbers written on the item.

20. When sales consultants move furniture on the showroom floor, it is their responsibility to put it back. Our stores are large and it may ruin the display in two vignettes for days.

21. Sales consultant must always use their full name when signing anything, no initials. Exception would be when keying in an invoice. You would use your assigned sales code.

22. All sales consultant must park in assigned areas. Areas are subject to change as business volume increases.

23. All sales consultants receive a back order report each week and are required to work their reports a minimum of three (3) times per week. Salespeople are required to notify customers when their merchandise has arrived.

SALES COMMISSIONS

1. Sales consultants are paid 4 percentage commission, weekly, on all delivered merchandise.

2. All sales consultants receive a commission report each week and should review it carefully. Any discrepancies should be written in proper form and submitted to the Sales Manager or Store Manager on Tuesday of each week.

3. To clarify any misunderstandings or assumptions, commissions are considered wages under Colorado's wage payment law. How or when a commission is earned, is governed by the employment contract. Your job description is the basis for computing the rate of pay and which an employment offer was made and has been accepted by you. Commissions are paid when they are "fully earned;" usually when the customer pays for the product or service, and has acknowledged acceptance and completion of said product or service. Adjustments to commissions will occur when required steps, forms and information is not completed fully by the sales consultant, thereby requiring the company to incur additional expense, time and labor to correct problems in order to meet the standards established for customer satisfaction and product or service acceptance.

4. We split commissions between stores when a customer provides the name of the sales consultant they worked with at the same store, another store or if the sale is a re-select.

SALES ETHICS

1. Stacking of customers at any time will not be tolerated. If a salesperson cannot close a customer, they must drop that customer clean. Do not expect to split the commission regardless of time spent with the customer. In leaving the customer, always say, "Anyone can help you." Never approach the customer if another salesperson is helping them. On very busy days it is okay to wait on more than one customer as designated by the Sales Manager. It is your responsibility to inquire of customers "Are you being helped by anyone?" Sales consultants should greet every customer in our store.

2. When a customer asks for a specific sales consultant, for a new purchase or reselect, you must make every effort to find that person. If they are unavailable the commission will be split. The sales consultant keying the invoice will enter their name (sales code) first.

3. Business cards are not to be given out until the customer is leaving the store at the front door or after they have completed their purchase at the front counter.

SALES POLICIES AND PROCEDURES

1. We accept Visa, Master Card, Discover, cash, or personal checks as forms of payment. Financing is also available through our credit department.

2. When bringing a customer to the cashier counter, have your invoices completed. The customer must sign their checks in the presence of a front office cashier. The front office personnel have specific policies they must follow in matching customers to their identification and to their form of payment. These policies are for the protection of the company and the customer.

3. We will hold merchandise two weeks if paid in full. We do not have a lay-away service. Management must approve any exceptions. CODs will be accepted on phone orders, back orders and special orders only.

4. Damaged or discontinued merchandise may be tagged and sold "1-only". This means the merchandise is sold "as-is, no warranty" but can be returned under the 30-day satisfaction guarantee. When keying the invoice, sales consultants are to use the "1-only" SKU under each item sold 1-only. To assist pullers in finding the merchandise, sold tags must be filled out completely and firmly attached to the merchandise and vignette numbers must be noted in <AC> Additional Comments. Sales consultants must

inspect the 1-only merchandise and not the damage in <AC> Additional Comments. We will not place plastic covers over sold merchandise on the sales floor.

5. All 1-only merchandise must be picked up with in 48 hours or delivered on the next available delivery date. Management must approve any exceptions.

6. Sold tags must include the customer's name, address, city, delivery date or pick-up date, invoice number, sales consultants full name (no initials) and date of sale. Improperly filled out sold tags will result in disciplinary action or commissions not fully earned.

7. Our store policy is to never be undersold! We will normally meet any competitors' prices (including Simmons bedding). Management must approve meeting a lower price or cutting a price for any reason. Sales consultants are to call and verify the selling price and the merchandise. Please report these occurrences to Jake Jabs, the Sales Manager, or the Buyer so they can adjust prices if necessary. Please confirm that the specifications are the same on the competitor's Simmons bedding before asking the Store Manager to match pricing.

8. We do not sell floor models unless approved by management. Occasionally customers will want merchandise off the floor. There are several reasons that you can give as to why we cannot sell floor models. All sales people are required to memorize the following five reasons we do not sell floor models:

- If we sold floor models you probably would not be looking at the furniture right now.
- The sales floor would look terrible.
- Can't sell against incoming purchase orders.
- Duplicate handling would result in higher prices.
- New merchandise is clean and in better condition.

9. Floor samples have been priced accordingly. Do not ask for an additional discount.

10. Our buyers and management strive to sell as much merchandise "open stock" as possible. However, some items must be sold as sets. Do not ask if merchandise that is priced as a group be broken up. Management has determined this already. If it can be sold individually or "open stock," it will be priced accordingly.

11. In referring to American Furniture Warehouse policies, never say "Jake's Policies." These are company policies developed by management.

Saying "Jake's Policies" infers that the customer can call Jake and get the policy changed. If a customer asks to see Jake on a sale, tell them Jake does not get involved in any sale.

12. Customers can check out fabric swatches and/or throw pillows with a $50 deposit. They must be returned within 24 hours or the customer will lose their deposit. This service is available Monday thru Friday only. Fill out fabric swatch/pillow check out form and take your customer to the front counter for them to pay their deposit. Filling out this form with a deposit is mandatory for customers wanting to take pillows or swatches out of the store.

13. We sell merchandise to many businesses; including child care facilities, medical offices, and restaurants. Furniture sold for business purposes (all Budget Value and sofa's under $400), will have a 30-day warranty. This must be made clear to the customer and the sales consultant is required to use the "30-DAY" SKU under each item. Sales consultants not using the "30-DAY" SKU are subject to suspension or termination.

14. Sales consultants selling to customers who are in the store late (near closing time) must stay until the customers have left the building. Problems may occur during load outs that require the

assistance of the sales consultant. A floor walk is required by each sales person at the end of their shift to identify any customers who may need assistance.

15. Casters on any entertainment center are for shipping purposes only. The customer must be advised to discard the casters or the merchandise will be unstable.

16. When a customer comes in to reselect different merchandise, check with customer service first or approval. Be sure to note in <AC> Additional Comments, the original invoice number and that it is a reselect. Always split the reselect invoice with the original sales consultants unless told otherwise by customer service or management.

17. Employees with 2 months to 5 years employment will receive a discount of 5 percent off the sale price. Employees with more then 5 years will receive a 10 percent discount off the sale price. The employee's manager must approve all discounts. Any abuse of these discounts will result in the loss of the discount and will be subject to personnel action. All employees are customers and should be treated as such. Commissions are paid on employee purchases. Sales consultants cannot write invoices on their own purchases.

18. Kit numbers cannot be back ordered, the computer will not acknowledge kit numbers and the back order will never be filled. Always key the individual SKU numbers that make up the kit.

INFORMATION TAGS

American Furniture Warehouse has created information tags to help customers understand the unique nature of certain products. These tags are attached directly to the merchandise for customer viewing and to remind sales consultants to explain the product thoroughly.

1. Budget Value - This merchandise comes with manufacturers' imperfections that are inherent in the mass production such as finish flaws etc. American Furniture Warehouse will give you its usual year warranty on the construction but cannot warranty the inherent imperfections.

2. Distressed Furniture - This furniture has been purposely distressed with the dents and rub marks that give it that "Antiqued" or "Old World" look. Here at American Furniture Warehouse, we want you to understand the nature of distressed furniture and the beauty it creates. The structure of this merchandise carries our usual one-year warranty.

3. Hand Made Furniture - This merchandise is hand made. Each piece varies in design and finish; it's part of the romance of buying hand made, hand carved & hand-finished furniture. Because most of it is made of solid wood, it must be oiled regularly in this dry mountain climate (including the underside of tables). Over a period of time, most solid woods will show weathering and cracks, which is part of the beauty of buying solid woods. This merchandise is covered under our usual one-year warranty, except for the weathering and cracks.

4. Fine Cherry Furniture - Nature signs every tree like a fingerprint with its own individual characteristics. These differences in grain pattern and color variation are the beauty of nature and add to the beauty, interest, and worth of fine solid woods, veneers and grained surfaces. Surface irregularities, small indentations and pockets in the wood are common in furniture made of cherry and cherry veneers. These are technically called sap or gum pockets. These are not defects but part of the beauty of cherry.

5. Solid Wood Furniture - When buying solid woods for your home, remember that stains penetrate into the wood grain and depending on the variables in the grain there will be different shading into the wood. Each piece of furniture will have different color shading so the piece you receive will be different than the floor model. This is the romance of buying solid

wood...it has character. In dry climates solid oak needs to be oiled regularly to keep it from splitting. Lacquered tables need to be oiled underneath regularly.

6. Metal Bunk Beds - Metal bunk beds come with manufacturers imperfections that are inherent in the mass production such as finish flaws, dents & scratches. American Furniture Warehouse will give you its usual one-year warranty on the construction, but cannot warranty the bending of metal due to jumping or other misuse.

7. Rusticos Furniture - Rusticos means "Rustic." This furniture is made from native lumber in the country of origin. To give it the Old World look, it is hand made. It is purposely made to look rustic. In dry climates like Colorado and Montana, it needs to be oiled regularly. This furniture will often crack, doors warp and hinges squeak... adding to its appeal and value. American Furniture Warehouse will give you its usual year warranty on the construction, but cannot warranty the cracking, warping and squeaky hinges.

Other tags are available such as "Pillow Top Comfort," "Natural Beauty of Leather," "Out of Stock," and "Just the Facts." These tags are to be maintained on the show floor by sales consultants.

SELLING BEDROOM FURNITURE AND BEDDING

1. We do not give away "free" bed frames. There is no such thing as a free bed frame. We pay for the bed frames from the manufacturer. If we gave away free bed frames, we would have to raise our prices to cover the cost of the free bed frames.

2. When selling bedroom furniture or bedding, sales consultants must indicate in <AC> Additional Comments if the customer does not need a bed frame. (NO FRAME NEEDED)

3. King and queen size Simmons products require bed frames with a rigid crosswise center support or at least 4 hardwood slats.

4. Simmons does not warranty their mattresses or box springs unless sold with matching mattress or box springs.

5. Sales consultants must key two box springs when selling king size bedding.

6. When selling bedding, particularly the pillow top mattresses, you can avoid customer complaints and returns if the customer is educated at the point of sale as to what to expect from their bedding and what is expected of them in maintaining new bedding. Body impressions in a new mattress indicate that the upholstery layers are conforming to the body's indi-

vidual contours. These are not defects but normal wear. Pillow top mattresses will not hold a rigid shape, as most ordinary mattresses will, due to the extra plush materials, which give the bed its comfort and softness. Sell this as a benefit. These impressions are going to be more noticeable on queen and king size mattresses. To equalize these impressions, advise the customer to turn the mattress upside down and end to end regularly every two weeks for the first three months and every three months thereafter.

7. Pillow top mattresses are sometimes as high as 36 inches. Sales consultants must show customers how high their bed is going to sit, with the measuring tools available. To compensate for beds that are too tall we sell low profile box springs and frames. When selling Pillow Top mattresses, "Pillow-Top discussed" must be typed into <AC> Additional Comments.

8. Queen split box springs are available in certain Simmons models to accommodate customers with narrow entryways and smaller rooms.

9. Like new shoes, the body may need time (up to 60 days) to adjust to sleeping on a new mattress. If a customer has been sleeping on a soft mattress, the body will quickly adjust to the extra support and sleeping comfort.

10. Customers should be advised to not fold or bend their mattress to fit through doorways and tight spaces.

11. Simmons queen and king size bedding are sold in sets. Customers wanting a mattress or box spring only in queen or king size will be charged 60 percent of the everyday price.

12. Customers should be made aware that some headboards need holes drilled and if they pick up the merchandise it is their responsibility to drill these holes.

13. Encourage customers buying wall beds to have them delivered. This will reduce customer exchanges and refunds.

SPECIAL ORDERS AND BACK ORDERS

1. Special orders are non-cancelable and nonrefundable, they must be approved by a manager and signed by the customer.

2. Special orders require a deposit of 50 percent on cash invoices and 20 percent on finance invoices.

3. Fabric, pillows and parts must be special ordered on a hand written purchase order and paid in full. All other special orders must be ordered in the computer using the correct special order SKUs.

4. Fabric can be ordered from any of our upholstery vendors for $25 a yard. One yard of fabric is 36" x 54" and the minimum order is one yard, no half yards.

5. Pillows can be special ordered for the following prices:

Small $ 15
Medium $ 25
Large $ 35

Sales consultant must indicate which sofa frame the pillow is being ordered from and determine the size of that pillow for pricing purposes.

6. Factory drop merchandise cannot be special ordered without the approval of the buyer. We will try to accommodate customers when possible, in order to complete their previous purchases.

7. Special ordering an entire sectional instead of individual pieces to match in stock pieces, will ensure consistent dye lot matching and will not create inventory problems.

8. Back ordered items must be keyed on a separate invoice from merchandise that is in stock and available for delivery.

9. The computer will automatically fill customer back orders and special orders when the merchandise is being received. In order for this to happen the "estimated delivery date" must be the same as the "date of purchase." If these dates do not match the customer's order will not be filled.

10. Sales consultants are not to back order accessory items.

11. When quoting shipping times to customers on special orders or back orders, it is absolutely vital that you do not mislead customers as to the arrival of their furniture. We do not guarantee special order shipping times or back order arrival dates.

12. Sales consultants are to quote back order dates and add approximately 14 days shipping time. The following statement should appear in the <AC> Additional Comments section on the customer's invoice. "SHIP DATE _____ ALLOW APPROXIMATELY 14 DAYS SHIPPING TIME." Special order shipping times are quoted from the "Factory Lead Time" sheet supplied to us and updated regularly by our special order department. The following statement should appear in the <AC> Additional Comments section on the customer's invoice. "ALLOW APPROXIMATELY ___ WEEKS SHIPPING TIME".

READY TO ASSEMBLE FURNITURE (RTA)

1. Sales consultants are to inform all customers that this merchandise takes a considerable amount of time to assemble.

2. American Furniture Warehouse does not assemble RTA furniture for the customer; neither do our employees on their own time. We will recommend an outside assembling company at the customer's expense. See the RTA department for details.

3. The RTA companies have 1-800 numbers for customers to call for parts and/or assistance in assembly. When a customer purchases RTA, they are to be given a list of these numbers. We do not stock parts for this merchandise, but the companies will respond to all inquiries and questions. Sales consultants can use the "SAUDER" SKU that prints the 1-800 number for Sauder Woodworking on the customer's invoice.

CUSTOMER SERVICE

1. American Furniture Warehouse offers a 30-day customer satisfaction guarantee if not completely satisfied. Customers returning merchandise after 30 days will be charged a restocking fee. This is not to be used as a closing tool by sales consultants.

2. Customer complaints must go to customer service, or the satellite store Manager. We have a fully staffed and competent customer service department. Customer service, or the satellite store managers will handle all deliveries, service calls, exchanges, reselects, etc.

3. Sales consultants must inform all customers to keep their receipt for warranties, exchanges, or repairs. When calling customer service with a complaint, the customer needs to have their invoice number ready to expedite the situation.

4. We must sell and deliver merchandise in our normal course of business, following our well-established procedures. Problems occur when we make exceptions to our procedures. In dealing with unreasonable or difficult customers that want the rules bent or broken, it is often better to cancel and refund than to cause a series of bad events.

5. It is imperative that you get an angry customer seated away from other customers. A loud, angry customer can upset everyone around them. Always remain calm and speak in a friendly, caring tone. Ask what the problem is and explain what you can do to help. Most of these situations will need to be turned over to the customer service department.

6. We only repair merchandise purchased from American Furniture Warehouse. The merchandise must be under our regular one-year warranty or extended factory warranty.

DELIVERY POLICIES

1. WE DO NOT OFFER FREE DELIVERY.

2. Our delivery charges are as follows:
   a. $20 minimum and $99 maximum for metro area.
   b. Under $1,000 is 6 percent of the purchase price, and over $1,000 is 5 percent of the purchase price, metro only.

c. Due to the costs of delivering to the Glenwood Springs and Pueblo metro areas the delivery fee for those metro areas are 7 percent of the purchase price under $1,000 and 6 percent of the purchase price over $1,000. The minimum is $30 and the maximum is $150. Mountain and outside metro deliveries are $1.50 per one-way mile or 5 percent of the purchase price whichever is greater. (Refer to delivery area sheet for more specifics.)

d. Mattress and box spring only deliveries are $10 per piece and $5 for the frame, metro only.

e. $30 for timed deliveries between the hours of 8 a.m. and 8 p.m., available 7 days a week, metro-only. Add the $300 charge to the regular delivery charge. Use the SKU "TIMED-DELIVERY" for all timed deliveries. Schedule all timed deliveries through the delivery department.

f. "Out of Town" deliveries indicate that we charge every time we deliver to that area.

3. Salespeople are to schedule metro deliveries, allowing one day between date of purchase and delivery date. Deliveries outside the metro area are to be scheduled using round trip in the order entry screen for the delivery days to that area. Use the customer's answer for mileage from our nearest store to their home to determine whether $1.50 per one-way mile

or 5 percent of the purchase price is greater for the delivery charge. Salespeople are never to schedule a delivery on the same day as a house closing.

4. Long distance deliveries in Colorado, Nebraska, Kansas, Wyoming, New Mexico, etc., need to be scheduled through the delivery department. These deliveries can take up to 30 days depending on the number of deliveries going to that area. Some out of state deliveries we cannot do during the winter months. When in doubt, check with the delivery dept.

5. We deliver approximately between 7 a.m. and 7 p.m., or until the delivery trucks are empty. Do not set an exact time of delivery. We will give the customer a 2 1/2 hour delivery window. Explain the following paragraph to customers that do not understand our delivery policies.

We sell over 20 million dollars of furniture a month and deliver thousands of pieces of furniture everyday from our central warehouse. Even with 110 trained drivers, 58 of the largest delivery trucks available, and a computerized routing system, it takes your understanding that requesting a morning or afternoon delivery is not possible.

However, we do offer a 2 1/2 hour delivery window. We will advise you of that time when you call the evening before your delivery at 303-286-9331 (outside metro Denver call 1-877-AFW-TRUCK or

1-877-239-8782.) If you should cancel or reschedule the day before your delivery, you will be charged a $25 cancellation fee. If you cancel the day of your delivery or are not home during your 2 1/2 hour window, you will forfeit your delivery fee and we will recharge to redeliver. We want to satisfy you, our customer. In order to do this lets work together to make the delivery of your new furniture a pleasant experience.

6. Our delivery charge does not include moving furniture around the customer's home. Sales consultant must tell the customer to have their rooms ready for the delivery. Our drivers work on commission and are not paid to move customer's furniture. If a customer needs something moved, a minimum charge of $5 will be charged. This fee depends on the size of the merchandise and the distance it needs to be moved. The <AC> Additional Comments section must be used to state whether or not this service is needed and to let drivers know exactly what is being moved. This service should be sold as a benefit. Customers can pay the drivers directly.

7. Our delivery drivers do not move, disconnect or connect customer's electronic equipment. This includes TV's, VCR's, stereos, computers, printers, etc. This information must be given to the customers buying entertainment centers, computer stands, etc.

8. It is very important to have complete addresses (including (N)orth, (S)outh, (E)ast or (W)est and Circle, Avenue, Place, etc.) according to Xata map routing procedures, and both home and work phone numbers. All delivery invoices must have a map page number with major cross streets, or directions in field #8 Delivery Instructions. Deliveries to apartments, condominiums, townhouses and mobile home parks must include, name of complex, building number and unit or lot number. A map or specific directions must accompany deliveries outside the metro area. Maps must be turned into the delivery dept. with a copy of the invoice.

9. We do not deliver accessory items (plants, rugs, etc.). We will deliver boxed lamps out of the warehouse, but the customer must be told that it will come boxed and unassembled. We will also deliver leaning mirrors.

10. When customers want items left in the original cartons or wrapping, the sales consultant needs to key in the "BOX" SKU under each item that needs to be left in the carton. Customer must also be informed that not all merchandise comes in a box, but we will wrap it in plastic if it does not come in a box.

11. When selling large sofas and king size mattresses, warn customers about possible delivery problems related to getting the merchandise in the home. Oversized sofas need at least a 36" doorway or

entrance to get through. If it is required that mattresses be bent, a disclaimer must be signed by the customer, and this is to be noted in "COMMENTS."

12. We DO NOT ship merchandise common carrier (UPS or US Postal Service) and we do not do any packaging for such shipments. Customers need to make all arrangements for packaging, pickup and shipping. The common carrier and the customer are responsible for all merchandise. Customers making these arrangements must be reminded that all warranties are Freight On Board (FOB) American Furniture Warehouse, Thornton.

13. Customers wanting to cancel an order scheduled for delivery must give us two days notice. Customers who cancel or reschedule the day before their delivery will be charged a $25 cancellation fee. If the customer cancels the day of delivery or is not home for the delivery, they will be charged a redelivery charge. This must be made clear to the customer by the sales consultant.

14. There is no COD's on deliveries or customer pick-ups. The exception is merchandise that is on back order, special orders or phone orders. Balances due can be paid by check with a valid drivers license or ID. Drivers can also accept Visa, Master Card, or Discover.

15. Sales consultants can solve most delivery problems at the point of sale plus maintain a good relationship with the customer. Sales consultants not explaining delivery policies correctly will result in commissions not fully earned.

OUT-OF-TOWN AND MOUNTAIN DELIVERIES

The following information should be thoroughly discussed with out-of-town customers:

1. We have a four-hour window for most out of town or mountain deliveries.

2. Our delivery trucks are 8 1/2 ft. wide, 45 ft. long, 13 1/2 ft. high and weigh approximately 13,000 lbs. empty.

3. Can our truck make it up your driveway? Is there a place where our truck can turn around once it reaches your house?

4. How steep is your driveway?

5. Are there any hairpin turns? If so, will our truck be able to make the turns? Remember, our trucks are 30 ft. long and the back end swings wide.

6. How wide is your driveway? Are there any ranches in the way? Will it be a problem if our truck breaks any branches?

7. Do you have any electrical wires, cables or tree branches lower than 13 1/2 ft.?

8. Is your driveway paved or gravel? If not, is there a possibility our truck will get stuck if muddy? Also, if muddy is there a problem if our trucks leave deep tire tracks in your driveway?

9. Are there any narrow bridges, ditches or dips in the road that would be a problem due to the weight and length of our trucks?

10. Will your driveway be accessible if it has snowed or is snowing?

11. If our truck cannot make it up your driveway, will you be available with a pickup truck to meet our delivery truck to unload the furniture?

LOADING DOCK POLICIES

1. If the customer is not satisfied with the new merchandise from the warehouse they have the options of taking the floor model, reselect or refund. The dock will not open several boxes to give the customer their choice.

2. Sales consultants will not tell the customer whether the merchandise is packed in a carton. About 70 percent of the furniture is now being shipped blanket wrapped to save carton and freight charges. We will plastic wrap if the customer prefers.

3. Do not tell customers the waiting time on the loading dock without checking first with the front office. Normal wait time is approximately 15 to 30 minutes.

4. We are physically unable to load out the hundreds of orders between 1 and 5 on Saturdays and Sundays. Sales consultants should remind customers of our extended hours and encourage them to pick up at other times to avoid long waits on the loading dock.

5. The loading dock closes at 9:30 p.m. every day.

6. Customers picking up merchandise at the main store warehouse with a COD balance must check in at the front office before going to the loading dock. Customers with paid in full invoices can go straight to the warehouse pick up desk for a dock door assignment. Dock doors 7 and 8 are designated for customer returns and even exchanges.

7. Do not tell customers what will or will not fit into their vehicle. We will not be responsible for loss/damage to vehicle or merchandise due to the loading or unloading of vehicles at the customer's request.

8. Remind out of town customers to check over merchandise on the dock to make sure there is no damage, they have all items purchased and hardware/assembly instructions are included.

RED CROSS PROCEDURES

We have a contract with Red Cross to help provide bedding and other essential items to victims of fire or other disasters. In order for American Furniture to receive payment, the following rules must be followed.

1. The customer must have a disbursing order from Red Cross.

2. Make sure the merchant name is American Furniture Warehouse.

3. Verify the customer's name.

4. There will be a description of what they can get and a maximum amount they can spend. They cannot get anything different from what is stated on the order. If the customer wants something different they must contact Red Cross and get a new disbursing order. The amount is a guideline. You do not have to try and use up all the money. Red Cross uses the guideline because they don't know our prices, and they don't want to pay over a certain amount. Note the amounts are for each item. They cannot use what they didn't spend on one item to get another item.

5. The following statement must be in the <AC> Additional Comments section: "Red Cross pays from this invoice. No statement will be sent". You will not charge tax. NOTE: The customer must sign both the disbursing order and the invoice.

6. If the customer cannot pick up the merchandise they need to pay for delivery.

MISCELLANEOUS

1. Upon leaving the company, a sales consultant will be paid on all of their sales as they are delivered. Weekly checks will be issued, but no draw paid. When it gets down to small amounts, under $100, checks may be issued every two or three weeks until all is paid.

2. Our TV spots and newspaper ads are available for customer viewing in each store.

3. When people ask where we get the animals for our television commercials, explain that they are rented from an out-of-town trainer.

4. Training tapes are available for viewing - e.g. Leather, Warehouse, and Front Office etc.

POLICY INTERPRETATION

All policies are subject to management interpretation. Management must approve any deviation. All sales consultants are expected to know, and are held responsible for, the material contained herein. Violations will be cause for personnel action. Severe or repetitious violations will result in suspension or termination.

35 KEY THOUGHTS

These principals are key to business success. Remarkable men have coined some of these phrases. But more than that, they've lived by them. Use these thoughts daily and you're bound to net the rewards you seek:

1. Fulfill a demand and you will be successful.

2. Be honest and you will never have to worry about what you said before.

3. Deliver value and service.

4. Live below your means.

5. Don't go into business just to make money.

6. Don't be afraid to sell for less than the next guy. Offer the best prices in town.

7. Business must offer value to society. It must not be simply a profit machine for the family.

8. Believe in the free enterprise system.

9. Believe the United States is the land of opportunity.

10. Believe we are living in the greatest time in the history of the world.

11. Get an education. This develops confidence and opens doors.

12. Develop an art form and hobbies. These will help you through troubled times.

13. Develop confidence in yourself. Organize your time, make a list, and move priorities to the top.

14. Keep physically fit; it helps your mental attitude.

15. Worry not about tomorrow because tomorrow will take care of itself.

16. It's ok to be a workaholic. Hard work is good for you.

17. Challenge yourself.

18. Be a risk taker.

19. Learn to say no.

20. Enthusiasm is contagious.

21. To achieve success you must swallow your ego.

22. If you enjoy what you are doing, you may never have to work a day in your life.

23. A successful person is one who does the task nobody else will do.

24. Keep your house in order.

25. To succeed you have to be willing to fail.

26. A great man is one who can walk with the common man but talk with kings.

27. Success is achieving what's important to you.

28. Be a good steward with what God has given you.

29. Don't love money. The love of money is the root of all evil.

30. Talk health, happiness and prosperity to every person you meet.

31. Ask not what your country can do for you, but what you can do for your country.

32. Competition is the spice of life.
It forces lower prices and delivers more value.

33. Small business-entrepreneurship is the lifeblood of America.

34. We must teach free enterprise, free market, entrepreneurship, and capitalism in our schools.

35. Get involved in your community.

PAY 'EM RIGHT

Finding employees to work for you, in a tight economy or when there are so many job opportunities that it seems no one wants to work, isn't rocket science. Pay more money. Our starting salary is $10.50 per hour. Plus, we offer an incentive program through which employees can make good money by busting their tails. When we opened our Pueblo, Colorado store we had 2,500 applicants show up the first day and 5,000 during the entire first week. The word was out that we paid more than other companies.

We recently started our own employment agency. We have a surplus of employees applying for jobs, especially in the clerical field. So we interview the candidates and then flip them to other companies located near us for a nominal fee.

So many companies complain about high turnover, the cost of training new employees, and the difficulty of finding good people. If they look hard enough, they'll find that the solution to their problems is right in front of them. Stop being penny wise and pound-foolish. Pay a little more up front, offer opportunity, and good employees will pay *you* dividends.

Jake jamming with
the Lawmen at the
Stockshow Jubilee
charity funtion.

JUST SAY NO

No interest, no payments promotion gimmicks are a definite no-no at American Furniture Warehouse. They are addictive to retailers and entrapping for the consumers. These no-no-no gimmicks that unimaginative retailers depend on are no better than heroin for drug addicts. Retailers get hooked and can't get off them; throwing themselves into a potentially downward promotional spin that saps them of marketing creativity and merchandising vigor.

Most retailers use these strategies because they can't think of more innovative ways to attract consumers. The pitfall is that once you suggest to your customers that furniture, delivery or financing is free you have backed yourself into a tight corner. What do you do for a promotional encore? Usually merchants just do more of the same. It's resulted in customers who have been dishonored and an industry that sports an embarrassing black eye.

There are many reasons to want to buy furniture. There's no need to suggest that furniture and services are free. Too many retailers send this message that's bound to get them instant gratification. But they fail to consider the long-term customer they are losing. This unnecessary entrapment drives people into debt and forces them to live beyond their means, unable to pay their bills. That's not the way to be a partner and friend to those you really want to be customers for life.

I believe in being honest and educating the customers. By explaining to customers that there is no such thing as free, we can win them over on honesty and value. We educate our American Furniture customers. If we offer no payments until some date in the future...no interest...or free delivery, we would have to raise our prices. The public is smart. The public understands that ultimately, the customer pays for all those extras in the form of higher prices.

So how do you break the cycle of no-no-no promotions? You create a plan and implement it. Do it cold turkey. Sure you may have a slow period, but in the long run, you will create a stronger image for your business and a more satisfied customer.

*Poolside antics at
Jake's fundraiser for
Astronaut Jack Schwigert.
Jack was elected to the
House of Representatives in
1985, but died shortly after
the election.*

Jake entertaining the kids at the Easter Seals Handicamp, July 1985.

GOOD GRIEVANCE

During my standard five-hour introductory lunch meeting with new employees, I ask them why it is they believe we have a grievance policy. Their responses are usually: "It's fair. It stops lawsuits." It's true. People are quick to sue today. They read about how someone spilled a cup of coffee in their lap at McDonald's and sued for a million dollars. I explain that this makes for great headlines, but that most papers don't print the second or third chapters of the story. A person goes through hell for several years and gets little or no satisfaction. The attorneys are the only ones who win.

So often you hear only one side of a dispute. You're ready to fire the other person, that is, until you hear their side of the story. Often the two stories are diametrically opposed. One salesman says that another salesman "stepped in and took my customer and I should get the commission on the deal." The other side is that it was the second salesman's customer. "The customer asked for me because I know the customer's house and I've sold to him before." We recently had a case in which an apartment buyer who has purchased hundreds of thousands of dollars worth of furniture from us came in to make a $30,000 buy. A new and greedy salesman tried to steal the sale. This not only upset the customer; it cost the company a lot of time and money. This large type of sale is complex; the furniture goes to multiple locations.

The set ups and delivery are complicated orders for a first-time salesmen. We pulled the commission on the new salesman and the situation went to Step Two in the grievance policy. The management team hearing the grievance decided to stick with the store manager's decision to pull the commission. We listened to all sides, talked to the customer and another witness to the sale, and we made our decision. The kind of person hearing a grievance in Step Two didn't get to that level unless they are fair and experienced in handling these types of situations.

The grievance policy gives us the opportunity to hear if we are doing something wrong. We can't fix a problem if we don't know the problem exists. We are a growing company and the bigger we get, the harder it is to communicate. This opens the door for an employee to register complaints. Sometimes we hire a little Napoleon or Hitler type manager, especially in our satellite stores. These managers intimidate employees who are afraid to complain. Because the grievance process is confidential, employees feel freer to register complaints.

Our grievance policy helps keep unions out. We are an anti-union company because of our experience with unions from 1975 until 1978. Immediately after I bought American Furniture in 1975, we had an election and I lost. The former American Furniture had four unions and one reason the owners were unable to sell the company and were forced to liquidate was due to the unions. Nobody was interested in buying a furniture company in Colorado with four unions.

My mistake was that I hired some of their employees, a warehouse manager, for example. I thought I was hiring the experience I needed but I also hired union organizers. We were a start-up company and didn't offer benefits like a 401(k). Unions often prey on start-up companies promising employees better salaries and better benefits. A business cannot promise anything not presently given to employees, and during the election period, employers are not allowed to promise them anything additional. This gives the union a definite competitive advantage. I lost the election. It only takes 51 percent of employees to win an election. To get the union out it takes three-fourths vote. I urge my employees today to avoid going to the union. Instead, use our grievance policy. We'll solve our own problems. We need to solve them ourselves. Tell us what our problems are so we can solve them.

We can solve any problem at American Furniture Warehouse, but first, we have to know that a problem exists. We can't fix it if we don't know it's broken. A lot of big companies fail at this because the CEO doesn't know what problems exist. Using the policy, portions of which are included below, we stay on top of our problems, and we can solve them:

26.0 GRIEVANCE POLICY

26.1 Grievances shall consist of all matters of disagreement arising out of the employer/employee relationship where there is no specific policy that clarifies the problem. This policy is not in effect for those employees who have been employed for less than ninety (90) days or have been terminated directly by the owner. To attempt resolution of a problem, employees *must* follow the specific steps outlined here:

STEP 1:

The employee discusses the complaint with his/her *immediate supervisor.* Normally, this should resolve the majority of work place problems. When these discussions do not resolve the differences or there is a personal or other reason you feel you cannot speak with your supervisor, you may go to the next step.

STEP 2:

The employee submits a written grievance to the *next level of supervision.* Five (5) copies shall be completed: The original to the CEO, one copy to the General Manager, one copy to the employee's supervisor, one copy to Personnel, and one copy must be kept by the employee. The written grievance must be presented within five (5) working days after the date of the immediate supervisor's decision. The answer by the Company must be given or mailed to the employee within ten (10) working days after receipt of the employee's appeal.

STEP 3:

If the decision in Step 1 is not acceptable to the employee or the owner, the case may be *appealed* in writing to an ad hoc grievance panel. The panel will consist of five (5) persons selected as follows: Two (2) members selected by the owner and two (2) members selected by the employee. The four (4) members will then select one (1) additional person to act as chairperson. The four (4) members and chairperson will arrange for a hearing and decide the case within a period of thirty (30) days after the appeal made in *Step 3.*

26.2 Any decision which is *not appealed* by the employee within the time allowed at each level after the date of receipt shall be considered a *decision in favor of the Company.* Any written grievance which is not answered by the company within the time allowed at each level after the date of receipt shall be considered a *decision in favor of the employee.*

SEX, LIES AND FALSE ACCUSATIONS

Sexual harassment is a considerable problem in business today. On a national basis, sexual harassment accusations and lawsuits are reaching epidemic proportions. In many cases, employees abuse the laws and the system and falsely accuse male employees for retaliation and to profit. Attorneys report that there are more than 5,000 sexual harassment cases in Denver right now. Some businesses buy insurance for sexual harassment. And a lot of people have learned that just by threatening a suit, the insurance company will pay them off. It's called blackmail. I say, "Stand up and be counted." If businesses back down and pay off accusers, it encourages blackmail.

What is most troubling is that laws that were passed to prevent harassment in the workplace are being abused. Employees and their lawyers use the threat of public exposure to shakedown companies and individuals. The system is being corrupted and many male and female business executives do not want to address the issue because they do not want to be portrayed as being politically incorrect.

My views are a result of a devastating personal experience. I was falsely accused of sexual harassment. The District Judge read her deposition and threw the case out of court, saying that no sexual harassment occurred.

The woman charging me with sexual harassment worked at our Fort Collins store. I only get to our Fort Collins store about every 60 to 90 days. The employee only worked for us 18 months. I had only spoken to her a few times, always with other employees around. I was never alone with her and did not ever harass her.

The problem started when I received a letter from an attorney. The letter charged that I had made repeated and continuous sexual advances, repeatedly fondling her, placing her in highly embarrassing personal situations, exposing myself to her, and committing battery against her. The letter alleged that American Furniture Warehouse and I were guilty of outrageous conduct resulting in emotional distress and, of course, violating her civil rights. She claimed that we created a hostile work environment in which she was forced to work and that she was discriminated against because she was female, in violation of Title VII of the Civil Rights Act of 1967. The charges went on and on.

The attorney wrote me saying his client wanted $75,000 to forget the charges. If I was unwilling to pay, the attorney threatened, he'd go to the press with the story. We wrote back refusing to pay. Then the attorney wrote again saying his client would take $40,000. At that time, my son-in-law and General Manager Brian Kurth urged us to pay the $40,000.

Jake on vocals at another charity function.

He took the position that if we didn't, the damage to the company would be devastating, especially once it hit the press. My celebrity status made it likely that the charges would get front-page coverage. Still, I refused.

Maybe Brian was right. Perhaps we could have negotiated the sum down even more if I had been willing. I believe you have to fight this type of blackmail. I'm not available for blackmail. When we wouldn't pay the woman off, she and her attorney went to the press with charges that made front page of *The Denver Post* and the TV and radio stations.

It was de-humanizing. The paper printed the phony accusations. The fact that the paper would print such accusations without a fair hearing makes me wonder about the manner in which the media operates. The accused are lynched in public, and later, when found innocent, the news is buried in the back of the paper.

Brian and my daughter, Terri, my upholstery buyer, left the company soon after the papers ran the story. I think one of the main reasons was the embarrassment of the lawsuit. My wife would not go outside of the house for months. I had to buy the groceries and go to the drycleaners, things she had always done. I, too, cut off going to charity functions and out in public. It was embarrassing and humiliating.

The extortion attempt didn't hurt our business. In fact, our business continued to grow and prosper. I learned through hundreds of letters and phone calls that there are many other people who have gone through the same ordeal. I received phone calls from individuals who would recall their case and start crying on the phone. Several teachers called to say they quit teaching because of the threat of sexual harassment charges. Some students, they said, trump up a false charge because of a disciplinary action meted out by the teacher. The teacher's name and reputation are ruined for life. Interestingly, these were both male and female teachers. Sports figures, too, are frequently targets for this kind of blackmail.

All too frequently employees use the laws to intimidate managers and to seek profit. The business environment is becoming increasingly dysfunctional because of the breakdown in behavior and communication between men and women. What is politically correct? What is correct or incorrect behavior? How does an employee defend himself or herself after being falsely accused?

Because of my case, we became aware of Background Information Services, Inc. (BIS) of Boulder. They track court cases and keep a data file on each one. One of their reps called me after reading *The Denver Post* article saying that the woman's name sounded familiar and if I wanted they would send their investigative report to me. That report listed 42 cases between her and her husband. He had beaten a murder rap in Oregon and they had a $100,000 judgment against him. They needed money desperately. Blackmailing me was one way to get it. American Furniture Warehouse started using BIS's services. We now do background checks on all our employees. Had we done this before, we probably wouldn't have hired my accuser and this whole thing wouldn't have happened.

The hundreds of people who called me have caused me to think about starting Harassment Victims Advocacy Group. I may yet. I know I would have lots of members. This sexual harassment charge will be with me the rest of my life, just as it will for the hundreds and hundreds of others who have been falsely accused.

On the following page is a letter I received from a man I don't know and have never met. But this letter explains a lot about how it can happen and what can be done:

August 2, 1995

Dear Senator Sally Hopper,

I'm sure you read the article about Jake Jabs of American Furniture Warehouse and the sex harassment charges by an "X" employee in The Denver Post last week. I do not know Jake, and have no opinion of his guilt or innocence. I do feel very strongly about the press's right to publish such a story when it is only a civil suit.

For $15, a person can file a civil suit, call the press...and get a million dollars of bad press on their former employer before an investigation of any kind is done. A criminal case is far different and requires lots of investigation before an indictment is issued. In other words, there is a check on credibility of the action. There is no check of the credibility of a plaintiff in a civil matter. To allow this to be news-worthy in our state is unjust. Many employees leave ...mad. Why should [an accuser] be allowed to cause this much bad press before any investigation is done? American Furniture employs hundreds of people. Should their jobs be at risk due to bad press for $15 before any investigation is conducted? Should Jake's business he has taken years to build be jeopardized without even an investigation or jury verdict? I don't think so!

Sex harassment suits and charges within companies are the in thing. They are about a dime a dozen now. In civil suit matters, I believe all people have the right to have it be a private matter until the jury decides the case. [A writer...] told me that's the law in England. I ask you to consider a law change in Colorado.

A constituent from Loveland, Colorado

The trial lawyers in Colorado and across the country are out of control. We need additional tort reform in Colorado. Plaintiffs and trial lawyers, who initiate lawsuits without basis, merely seeking to secure a profitable out-of-court settlement, should absorb the entire costs of all legal expenses when their suit is thrown out. We need additional laws passed in Colorado that address prejudgment interest and fiduciary duty because Colorado judges have issued rulings that weaken previously passed tort reform legislation.

I plan to serve as the new President of the Colorado Civil Justice League, the new organization affiliated with American Tort Reform Association. Our goal is to create a vigorous agenda to halt this runaway situation. It's costing Americans millions of dollars not to mention ruining the reputation of individuals and businesses.

*Jake and Ann Jabs
with Charlton Heston—
taken at a 1984 election
year fundraiser.*

POLITICAL ANIMAL, NOT

I tested the waters for the U.S. Senate seat for Colorado in 1985. As long as you don't spend $5,000, it's called testing the waters. Once you spend $5,000, you must announce your candidacy and you are given a thick book of rules you need to follow.

An AP reporter from Estes Park, Colorado interviewed me. She was enthralled with the idea of a businessman entering the political arena. It was during the Reagan years and there was a real interest in politics by businessmen everywhere. At this same time, "Term Limitations" were being talked about. Many constituents had tired of the professional politician. The push was on to run government like a good business instead of a welfare state. Once this reporter's story appeared, nearly every major newspaper picked it up off of the wire. I got calls from across the country, plus some donations to my campaign.

What I didn't realize was that it wasn't my turn to run for the U.S. Senate seat. In politics, you have to wait your turn. You have to pay your dues and wait your turn. You need to start by going to precinct meetings and walking the streets to become precinct captain. You work your way up becoming a county commissioner, mayor, representative, and city or state auditor. The party doesn't appreciate outsiders. Nearly every politician would like to become a senator or even President of the United States. Understand that even a wealthy businessman doesn't short-circuit the process. The party chooses the candidate.

It was Ken Kramer's turn. He was a six-term U.S. Representative to Congress from the 6th District. Martha Ezzard, a State Senator, and Terry Considine, U.S. Senator Bill Armstrong's campaign manager, ran against Kramer. Both Ezzard and Considine were shut out at the State Convention. I, too, would have been shut out at the convention.

Kramer ultimately lost the election to Tim Wirth.

I did not spend $5,000, so I never announced I was running. But I was getting national publicity as well as local. In the end, I'm glad I didn't run. The late '80s were bad years for Colorado. Politics takes a lot of time. And I believe now that my business would have folded had I run. Plenty of successful businesspeople go broke after getting into politics.

The trouble with politics is you have to learn to give different speeches. If you're talking to a conservative group, you have to have one speech. If you're talking to a liberal group, you give another speech. You can't say what you really think. You have to be wishy-washy on many issues. You are cornered on issues like abortion, gun control, and often take the popular side rather than what you believe in. Those who know me understand I'm very outspoken. I would not have the stomach nor the patience for politics. I've called my own shots since I was 24 and you can't do that in politics.

In politics, there is only one winner. As many as eight to 12 people run for a single office and only one wins. All other candidates lose. Broken egos, disappointment, and often hard feelings result. A joke that circulates in political crowds says it all: When making introductions to a crowd, it's common to hear, "All those not running for office stand up." That's a more manageable crowd than those who are running.

Jake as
Celebrity Guest Host.

BE CHARITABLE, WISELY

I have a storewide policy that if someone walks in asking for a donation to a charity or a cause, I just give it to him or her. You don't know how special it makes people feel-a Girl Scout, Boy Scout, a high school student selling ads in their yearbook, a person soliciting an item for an auction, someone injured in an accident, a person who has cancer, or one whose house burned down. Just give them what they ask for. Sometimes I'll donate a gift certificate for furniture, and almost always they buy more than the certificate. I broke even; but they feel special. And it always makes me feel good too.

We get a lot of requests for furniture and mattresses to help the homeless or a shelter. We just give it to them. It comes off your entire inventory, so you don't have to argue with the IRS about the donations. We gave furniture to everyone who lost his or her furniture during the Ft. Collins flood. We gave office furniture to Easter Seals and Make a Wish. Easter Seals recently named the dining room at the Rocky Mountain Handi-Camp "Jake's Place." I didn't ask for anything in return.

But I do have my limits. I believe in helping people who are handicapped or disabled, those with Multiple Sclerosis, Muscular Dystrophy, or cancer-charities that help people as well as do research to cure some of these diseases. I don't give to the symphony orchestra or art shows. In my opinion these entities should not operate as a charity. If there is enough demand for their services, they can support themselves. If not, they should go out of business.

We give to more than 300 charities a year, not including a lot of the small walk-in requests. One of our biggest charitable efforts is an annual 56-hour Labor Day sale from which we donate 2 percent of our gross sales to help Jerry's Kids. It raises over $100,000 now, but when we started, it only raised $7,000. It's a great promotion and the Muscular Dystrophy Association loves it. The MDA poster child visits us and we feature the child on TV commercials. It calls attention to the telethon and conveys a positive image to the community. We do the same thing in March with Easter Seals. This is a great charity with 95 percent of the money going to help the disabled. I don't, by the way, give to the United Way; they have big offices and high-priced executives.

When I first started doing commercials the phone started to ring off the hook with people asking for donations. So I hired a secretary and had her check out the merit of each charity. What I found was that the big national charities normally spend 10 percent or less in operating costs. One reason for that is that they raise a lot of money, so their operating costs become a small percentage of the total. I like to find the charities that direct most of the money for those who need it, or to those performing research, instead of giving to charities with excessive overhead costs.

I don't always give to get publicity. If it comes with the gift it's okay, but sometimes I get more out of giving to a good cause because I truly believe in giving back. Over the years, I have probably gotten as much personal satisfaction out of what I've given as the value of what I gave.

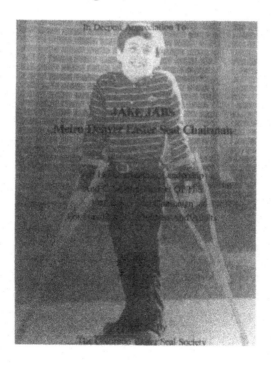

Grandson Joel,
daughter Kim,
granddaughter Katrina,
Jake and one
of the kittens.

LEARNING LATER

I'm sorry to say I have not been able to do a good job of getting along with family. I'm referring to my immediate family. The extended Jabs family gets along well and we have a sibling get-together every year and a big Jabs family reunion every three years. We convene at a campsite in the mountains of Montana where we gather around the campfire and sometimes sing all night. We play volleyball, horseshoes, and just plain sit around and visit. We have a good time. There's never really been a problem with my brothers and sisters.

But with my own children, I made mistakes. Frankly, I got them into the business too soon and gave them part of the business too soon. I've attended too many seminars about passing the business to your family. These experts talk a great deal about the tax and inheritance ramifications, but very little about the human impact. I think the furniture trade publications—going out to so many family owned businesses—push this notion of succession from a tax point of view far too much. I've also listened to business planners who suggest giving stock in your company while it is growing so it will bypass estate taxes. Once again, they were looking at the financial implications, not the human ones.

It didn't work for me. I gave the kids early retirement and I'm still working.

I've learned from experience that family members should work outside the business for years before going to work for a family business. That way they learn what the real world is about along with other job skills. Then if they want to join the business they will appreciate it more and will also bring to the table other job skills they've learned elsewhere. If I had it to do over again, I wouldn't have hired them until they were 25 years old. And I'd wait until son-in-laws are 30. Plus, I wouldn't have given them stock or property for another 10 years, and only after they earned it.

Sometimes we learn the hard way, even after achieving success.

Jake & Ann Jabs Wedding,
February 8, 1960.
Bozeman, Montana

*Jake Jabs accepting the
Retailer of the Year Award
from Hershel Alpert,
Chairman of the NHFA.*

RETAILER OF THE YEAR 2000

On April 6, 2000, Jake Jabs was presented with the most prestigious award of the furniture industry, the National Home Furnishings Association (NHFA) Retailer of the Year for 2000. The honor was presented to him at a ceremony in High Point, North Carolina during the Spring International Home Furnishings Market.

The award recognizes outstanding contributions to the home furnishings industry, exemplary service to the community, and personal business achievements. Nominations for the NHFA's Retailer of the Year are solicited from every segment of the industry, including more than 10,000 retailers, manufacturers, factory representatives, and the press. The selection committee is comprised of retailers, NHFA sponsor manufacturers and suppliers, a principal of the International Home Furnishings Representatives Association, and a member of the home furnishings press.

The community of Colorado, citizens and elected officials, as well as Jab's peers, and the directors of various Denver charities rallied in support of his nomination. Colorado Governor Bill Owens praised Jabs' for his exemplary service to the community. "His willingness to serve others has not only brought prosperity to his business, but also made Colorado a better place to live. Jake Jabs brings integrity to his industry and is a true leader in his community," Governor Owens said.

"Jake Jabs was an excellent choice as the first recipient of this award in the new millennium," Hershel Alpert, NHFA Chairman, said. "He has been a leader in all aspects of retailing from his insistence upon truthful furniture tags to innovative and humorous TV commercials featuring exotic animals. He has raised the bar for the entire furnishings industry by creating educated, informed customers."

Part of the nomination packet was an explanation of Jab's personal crusade to improve customer service by getting factories to ship parts within 24 hours. In reference to these efforts, John Wampler, President and CEO of Pulaski Furniture, said, "Simply put, Jake Jabs has helped the people at Pulaski Furniture and his many other suppliers do their jobs better."

"He is a complete person who truly cares about people, especially children, and has definitely made a difference in the lives of others through his unselfishness, integrity and warm heart," said Shirley Barenberg, Vice President of Development for Easter Seals Colorado.

On Wednesday, April 12, 2000, the Colorado Legislature presented Jabs with a proclamation for his service to the community. Majority Leader Doug Dean read the proclamation on the floor of the House of Representatives to a full room of fellow legislators, American Furniture Warehouse employees, and the media. Governor Owens also honored Jake Jabs proclaiming April 12, 2000 as "A Day In Honor of Jake Jabs."

Jake receiving the Proclamation from the Senate and House of Respresentatives at the Colorado State Capitol.

Honorary Proclamation

BILL OWENS
GOVERNOR

A DAY IN HONOR OF JAKE JABS
April 12, 2000

WHEREAS, Jake Jabs received the 2000 Retailer of the Year Award presented by the National Home Furnishings Association on April 6, 2000 for his outstanding contributions to the home furnishings industry, his honorable services to the community as well as his personal business achievements; and

WHEREAS, Jake Jabs exemplifies the American ideal as an entrepreneur, salesman, motivator, and humanitarian who upholds both a strong work ethic and family value; and

WHEREAS, American Furniture Warehouse has supplied corporate sponsorships, volunteer speaking and community service to the following organizations: Muscular Dystrophy Association, Easter Seals, Make-A-Wish Foundation, Toys For Tots, Children's Diabetes Foundations, American Heart Association, Arthritis Foundation, Alzheimer's Foundation, and the Rocky Mountain Youth; and

WHEREAS, Jake Jabs has been the recipient of numerous important awards such as the 1981 Presidential Achievement Award, and the 1984 Furniture Industry Humanitarian Award, 1994 Entrepreneur of the Year Award, and the 1999 Western Retailer of the Year Award; and

WHEREAS, Jake Jabs personifies the American dream, and has brought Colorado to compete on a global level, and helped retain a stable and growing economy;

Now Therefore, I, Bill Owens, Governor of the State of Colorado, do hereby proclaim April 12, 2000, as

A DAY IN HONOR OF JAKE JABS

in the State of Colorado.

GIVEN under my hand and the Executive Seal of the State of Colorado, this eleventh day of April, 2000

Bill Owens
Governor

KUDOS

Over the years, Jake Jabs and American Furniture Warehouse have received numerous awards and honors from a variety of organizations, business groups and associations nationwide.

Western Retailer of the Year - 1999
(Western Home Furnishings Association)

Retailer of the Month, Simmons Company - April 1998

National Vice President for MDS 1997-1998

Award of Excellence from *Furniture Today* - 1997

Citizen of the Year Award - 1997
(North Metro Denver Realtor Association)

National Buyer Appreciation Award - 1996
(Tupelo Furniture Market)

95 Top Retailers to Watch in 1995
(*Furniture Today* magazine)

Company of the Year - 1994
(Presented by Colorado Association of Commerce and Industry, *Colorado Business*, and Coopers & Lybrand)

Retailer of the Year Finalist - 1994
(National Home Furnishings Association)

Entrepreneur of the Year - 1994
(Presented by Channel 9 News, the *Denver Business Journal*, Merrill Lynch, Inc., and Ernst & Young)

Edgar "F." Daddy Allen Award - 1994
(Presented by the Colorado Easter Seal Society as its
most prestigious award for its 75th Year Celebration)

Top 25 Who Made It Happen in 1994
(*Furniture Today* magazine)

Voted Best Furniture Store Readers' Choice Award -
1994-Present (*Rocky Mountain News*)

Major Financial Contributor on an Annual Basis
1981 - 1994 (Helping to broadcast Easter
Seals Telethons)

Easter Seals Telethon Co-Host 1984-1990

Included in *Colorado's Who's Who* publications - 1990

Who's Who Award - 1990

Entrepreneur of the Year Finalist - 1990

Easter Seals Volunteer of the Year Lily Award - 1989

Furniture Industry Humanitarian - 1984

CARE Award, Businessman with a Heart - 1982

American Legion Community Service Award - 1982

Presidential Achievement Award - 1981

Montana Small Business Person of the Year - 1981

Colorado Veteran of Foreign Wars Citizens Award -
1980

Muscular Dystrophy Association - 1975-Present (Contributions of more than $1 million achieved through donating a percentage of sales)

Multiple Sclerosis Volunteer of the Year

U.S. Health and Human Services Award

Humanitarian Award by F.U.R.N. Club

Supporter of Boys and Girls Clubs, Boy Scouts of America, DECA, and hundreds of other charities each year

Jake, President George Bush
& Senator Hank Brown of Colorado.

Jake and Reba McIntyre at fundraiser.

*Jake with Jack Kemp
and Jack Schwigert.*

Jake and Freddie Fender.

Jake bullriding in front of the store.

TO ORDER MORE BOOKS...

To order more copies of:
  AN AMERICAN TIGER
  JAKE JABS-AN AUTOBIOGRAPHY,
please fill out the order form on the next
page and mail it to:
  American Furniture Warehouse
  Book Offer
  8501 Grant Street
  Thornton, Colorado 80229

Please fax orders to:
  303-853-4129

Or, order online at:
  www.afwonline.com or
  www.jakejabs.com

All book proceeds are donated to charity.

ORDER FORM

Name: _____

Company: _____

Address: _____

_____

_____

Phone: _____

Fax: _____

# of Copies @ $19.99 each _____

add $2.50 shipping and handling _____

Subtotal _____

Colorado residents add
3% sales tax _____

Total _____

Method of payment:

❏ MasterCard   ❏ Visa   ❏ Discover

Card Number: _____

Expiration Date: _____

Signature: _____

Check: _____ Other: _____

From Small Montana Farm,
To Leading American Retailer

NHFA's
Retailer
of the Year
2000

The prestigous Retailer of the Year Award is presented annually at the Spring International Home Furnishings Market in High Point, North Carolina. The recipient is selected for his/her outstanding contributions to the home furnishings industry, exemplary service to the community and personal business achievements.